WILL WORK FOR APPLES

WILL WORK FOR APPLES

THE TEACHER'S PETS

INTRODUCTION

I think motherhood is the toughest job in the world, but coming in a close second would have to be teaching.

Teachers are either freaking saints or they're crazy. Many of my closest friends are teachers and I still can't decide.

You'd have to be crazy to choose to spend all day trying to shape and mold young kids. I barely want to hang out with my own kids, I definitely don't want to hang out with someone else's kids!

But when I think about what they're paid, I think they must be saints. Teachers willingly take the job knowing their salary won't even cover their student loans. There aren't bonuses for teachers unless you count all the apples, scented candles, Best Teacher mugs, sweaty hugs, and cold germs they receive every year.

At some point in our lives we've had a teacher who made an impact on us. A teacher who went above and beyond to reach us. A teacher who changed us. A teacher who saw us and heard us. Those are the ones we remember and those are the ones we dedicate this book to.

Jen Mann

1

Dear Rachel: Letter to a First-Year Teacher
By Erin Dymowski

Dear Rachel,

Welcome to the club, newbie! The ink on that teaching certificate is still a little wet, but here you are with your pristine new planner, shiny new pens, and bright eyes full of optimism ready to be that thing you have written on your heart: a teacher. As your mentor, I need to give those rose-colored glasses of yours a little adjustment, even if that means pulverizing them into dust on the floor. What's coming next is going to be the hardest year of your life. You rocked your college classes and your student teaching, but actually teaching is the next level. The complicated truth of what teaching really is and what it will require of you will dissolve your idyllic fantasies at the door. If you are anything like the rest of us though, you'll survive mostly intact, live to tell the tale, and fall head over heels in love with this crazy profession in spite of it all. If you are really lucky, you might even get to share your love story with another fresh-faced newcomer.

You have already received this message loud and clear, but it bears underlining and highlighting: This job is not going to be what you expected. For starters, your students will not resemble the sweet-and-saccharin concoctions of Disney fare. Children are humanity in all its beauty and savagery, without any of the careful constructs of civility. You may have sensed that kids were unpredictable, sneaky, and wholly averse to adult direction during your teacher preparation. What you won't know until it smacks you in the face is the depths of their ruthlessness. They will totally sell you down the river to their parents or your principal if it keeps their butts out of hot water. Feelings of murderous rage toward the conniving little manipulators are totally justified. But, and this is an important but, not all kids are like that. Some of them will really need you to explain, coach, and inspire them. Others will just appreciate you as a friendly face on their journey. Some will give you a great story to tell or a funny anecdote to pull out at a cocktail party. But there will be those kids that imprint on you for the way they touched your life. The kids who bring baggage that is way too heavy for such small people to carry will change your worldview forever. The ones who challenge or delight or weasel their way into your own story will change, well, you. Welcome them all in your classroom. Make your space the safe place to land.

As you may have guessed, this year's emotional roller coaster is not for sissies, so stock up on chocolate and sad movies now in anticipation of the catharsis you will require every weekend. Your old Netflix account might get a little tired as you let yourself weep for the kids who break your heart. But you'll also shed a couple for the little creep who ruins your lesson plan every day and even the problem child who terrorizes other students. You'll go through boxes of tissues for your casually cruel bullies, your anxiety-ridden strivers, your attention-grabbing clowns, and your gifted students alike. But wait, don't forget your students with learning disabilities, emotional problems, gender dissonance, drug abuse, sexual abuse, and well, the list goes on and on. The truth is that you're gonna cry for all of them.

From the second their name hits your roster, they are yours in ways that a momma bear would totally understand: "Yeah, that one's a hot mess, but he's my hot mess." You might mourn all the lost time with friends and all the dates you had to reschedule because you are constantly changing lesson plans and dealing with behavior issues, but mostly you will cry because you will feel inadequate. Your worst days aren't going to tank the market or cause an international skirmish, but they might teeter on the edge of soul-crushing for one of your kids and that really hurts to think about. That's not what you signed up for. You are a girl who loves freshly sharpened pencils and the smell of new books and a rainbow stack of Post-it notes. You wanted the made-for-TV version of this job or a chance to be like Mrs. Meadows, who really saw you in math class in tenth grade or Ms. Neff who told you that you had the heart of a writer. That's what you thought you were getting. This is what you got. That's why we add the wine to the Netflix marathon.

It's not that your students will defy your expectations so much as make you completely re-evaluate why you had any at all. When you are preparing to teach, there's only talk of strategies and pedagogies and management systems, but not nearly so much of the many needs to meet and the little time to meet them. That's a real shame. Nobody felt the need to explain that while in fact you are not a social worker nor a guidance counselor, priest, circus performer, magician, or Mary Poppins-esque character, you might have a better chance at this job if you had a hefty helping of any or preferably all of those things.

Have heart though. There is so much gold to be found among the rubble. First and foremost is the gift of your fellow teachers. Teachers are the ultimate can-do crowd. Be prepared to get inspired daily by the lengths they will go to help a child, the creative solutions they manufacture on the fly, their literal hunger for knowledge, the depths of their love for humanity. These are the folks perpetually unafraid to tackle life's messes and turn it into something manageable, thoughtful, and even beautiful. They have made careers out of trying to do this. They are more than willing to share their secrets with you: friends in the foxhole are the very best kind. Second is the very nature of the job itself. Teaching is no boring desk job. In fact, collectively, we represent a crew who would probably wither and die in a cubicle. Yeah, we grade and plan and plan some more, but despite what your professor might have told you, those lesson plans were made to be broken. Great teaching, the kind that hooks us and keeps us coming back for more, happens off script. So follow your instincts and ask the question on the tip of your tongue, rile the class up a little, push them a little further every day, play with them. These subtle moves are the ones that will pay you back in terms of reconciling the reality in front of you with the vision that brought you here. Third, you are already too far in to turn back now anyway. Teachers aren't just made; they are called. The truth is that you are talented, hard-working, and ambitious. You seemingly have a whole world of options laid out before you. You and I both know though that, in the end, there is only one: this path, this place, this profession.

Teaching almost always delivers on this promise. Every day, every week, every month, every year, as a job, teaching is engaging and fulfilling, not just because your kids grow and change, but because you do. So go ahead and stay late, wring yourself out, and even cry a little. Lay yourself prostrate at the feet of this holy mountain you are trying to climb. Teaching is a very real vocation, so take all the higher power metaphors you can get. Remember that you are not just teaching someone how to write a sonnet or calculate algebraic equations; you are teaching someone how to "human." That calls for some serious rolled-up-sleeves-level work, even if you are served some powerful helpings of humility in the process,

Find comfort in the knowledge that we need you here, we want you here, and most importantly, you deserve to be here. With your new ideas and unvarnished vantage point, you don't just remind us of where we came from, you actually help us get where we need to go. So much of teaching is becoming the lead learner. Just glean what you need from what is in front of you whether it's the curriculum, the kids, your fellow teachers, or even the messiness of the danky swamp that is this year. Try to see it as beneficial, the fertile ground for cultivating your personal teacher groove. Despite all the headaches and heartaches, when you pack your things for the summer, you will not just have a file cabinet worth of material, you will have the confidence that only comes from competence. Think of your second-year teacher swagger as the gold star for wading through the morass of this first year.

But no more pep talk, friend, because now you have got to go home. No, seriously, get your sorry new teacher butt home. Watching the sun rise and set from inside a school building is no way to keep your wonderful spark alive. School is a marathon not a sprint and not just for your students. You still shine with the excitement of your first class, and that's a good thing for us old and slightly jaded teachers to see. You are still in thrall of all the trappings of teacherdom—the school supplies, the grading scales, even the bulletin board I "Tom Sawyer"-ed you into putting up for me. There will always be paperwork and boards to cover and tests to grade. The paradox of teaching is that the other parts of it that might break your heart a little are also what makes it great.

In the end, as your mentor, if I can give you anything, I hope it's the courage to do this all again tomorrow and all the tomorrows after that until you have the successful and fulfilling career you deserve. All the elements you need to be a success in this job you already have. But here's one more thing I need you to hear. My first year teaching I shared a room with a teacher who had a framed cross-stitch on her desk. Small, crudely pieced together, and thrown in a cheap frame, it read "connection over content." Teaching has never just been about diagramming sentences or quadratic equations or ancient history. This thing we are doing is noble and fine and a damn good way to spend a lifetime. In the end, we teach best that which we need to learn. We, as humans, are all in need of touching the essence of what makes us so. Being a teacher just means you get a chance to give it a go every day. Welcome to the tribe, Rachel, but now you need to get yourself home.

Fondly,

E

. . .

ERIN DYMOWSKI IS A MOTHER OF FIVE, A TEACHER TO MANY, AND A WRITER WHEN SHE HAS A MINUTE. SHE WRITES WITH HER FRIEND ELLEN WILLIAMS AT SISTERHOOD OF THE SENSIBLE MOMS. HER WORK HAS BEEN FEATURED IN *THE HUFFINGTON POST*, HONORED AT BLOGHER, AND FEATURED IN SEVERAL ANTHOLOGIES. ERIN CURRENTLY TEACHES STEM IN GRADES ONE THROUGH EIGHT, AND SOCIAL STUDIES TO SIXTH-GRADERS. HER JOB HAS MADE HER FLUENT IN FORTNITE, HOW TO MAKE SLIME, AND THE COOLEST MEMES. SHE FEELS FORTUNATE THAT THIS PROFESSION FOUND HER DESPITE ALL THAT. SHE FEELS EVEN MORE FORTUNATE SHE FOUND SOME WORDS TO SHARE A LITTLE OF HOW SHE FEELS ABOUT IT.

2

What I Like Best About Latin
By Megan Sullivan

I could never tell what I liked best about Latin. It might have been the mythology mural that splashed across the entire wall near my desk, the ever-growing assortment of gel pens and scented hand sanitizer that populated the shelves, or the corner with the Keurig and college mugs where I made myself hot apple cider while we checked homework, all the things that made this classroom the only interesting place in this prison of a school building. It might have been the tests, served to us on neon paper in every color but lime, since you couldn't look at it for too long without burning your eyes, and accompanied by the most random of bonus questions ("Name the king and queen of Troy and the two instruments my son plays") and candy bribes when we complained too much. Maybe it was the fact that I was really and truly good at this, and my pride when classmates immediately deferred to me for help, or the realization a month into my first year that I was reading another language—a dead one, at that!—which was something very few other eighth-graders could say.

The common thread, of course, is my Latin teacher, Mrs. Camp-bell, who has put up with me for an astounding five years of classes, five class trips, ten days in Italy, and hours worth of Latin Club and Honor Society meetings. She's written my recommendations for college, two scholarships, and three other programs; I've owed almost every opportunity I got in high school to her. I live out of her class-room during lunch, study hall, and before school—and despite this being a high enough dose of Megan to exhaust anyone, she *still* answers my grammar meme texts. And she might have to deal with even more of me in the future, because I'm going to become a Latin teacher too.

IT'S VERY hard to form a close relationship with anyone at a secondary school of four thousand students unless you find a niche, so after a floundering seventh-grade year, I found Latin and clung to it. I picked the language partially because I could never hope to pronounce French or to write Chinese, partially because I was deeply absorbed in Harry Potter and Percy Jackson, and partially because I have always been the exact kind of nerd to choose this. And I found the exact kind of people I was looking for in Latin; everyone was *crazy*.

In eighth grade, I began my first Latin class at once eager and anxious. The promise of a new language excited me—so much more promising than the lagging pace of my English class or the insur-mountable challenge of geometry—but it was something I had never tried before, and I had a nagging worry that I might not be good. Apart from math class, I was used to understanding academics, and I didn't know what to make of this new terrain.

And I had no idea what to make of the class itself. The first thing I saw in the classroom was a stop sign warning me to not enter unless I had homework for Magistra Campbell, which sent me into a silent panicky spiral. Was she strict about homework policies? Oh God, I am a mess about homework, am I going to fail Latin and ruin my high school GPA already? And what does Magistra mean, anyways? Is that, like, Latin for *señora*? How do you even *pronounce* that? (She was not strict about homework, as I ascertained by skipping it for most of Latin III; I did not fail Latin in the slightest; it means teacher; hard G. Beyond this falsely intimidating sign, the classroom was strewn with Doctor Who merchandise and glitter gel pens, a blaring contrast to the stark whiteness of the rest of the school. The wall near the door was fully covered with a mythology mural; I sat as close to it as possible, hoping to absorb some of the brightness to get me through the rest of my school day.

The morning bell rang and immediately the teacher was yelling at us. Or no, not yelling—she just talked like that, in a permanent bouncing caps lock. "OKAY, WELCOME TO LATIN, KIDDOS!"

It was only 7:20 a.m., and Mrs. Campbell was shouting like she was her own megaphone. I wondered anew if I should be afraid.

After the standard introduction PowerPoint and syllabus, we were ready to be thrown into the deep end and begin speaking our own Latin, a very formulaic back-and-forth of hello and how are you. This was it, my first chance to prove myself! Drilling into my head that the Vs are always pronounced like W, I wandered around the classroom, accosting high schoolers with a chipper *salve*, guarding my glance so that it didn't cop out and drift to the board.

"You have this memorized already?" a girl asked me a couple minutes into the exercise with some surprise.

"Yeah?" I replied casually, channeling Elle Woods' "What, like it's hard?" It was only Latin. No big deal.

But it *was* a big deal. I'd survived my introduction small talk with ease, something I struggled with in English, and I was good at it too! I stood out here. I could do something. And in middle school, I needed that refuge.

Latin became my thing. I could understand a whole new language, which thrilled me to no end, but I also loved the steady chaos of the class. While English would try to kill me inside with plot charts and book reports, and PE ground my self esteem down with every lap I ran, Latin was reliably a good time. In between the vocabulary and grammar drills, Mrs. Campbell would squirt sleeping students with a spritz bottle as if we were misbehaving cats, take us outside to practice verbs in sidewalk chalk, and roll her eyes as we giggled over a textbook character named Sextus.

As any middle schooler might, I became wrapped up in my new hobby to the point of being kind of an asshole about it. I read ahead in the textbook so that I'd look smart in future classes, I delighted in my classmates relying on me for homework help, and I performatively read Percy Jackson over and over again. It would have been very easy to knock me down a peg or two to deflate my arrogance and make me a little more palatable, but Mrs. Campbell never did. She let me have my thing and delight in being smart, which got me through a lot of eighth grade.

In ninth grade, I had a different teacher for Latin II, so I assumed things were over between Mrs. Campbell and I, and that I would move on. Early that September, I saw her in the hallway and gave a little wave, then moved on. The next day, she accosted me in the same spot with mock offense that I hadn't even said hi. I decided that things probably weren't over then.

Latin III is traditionally known among Latin students as the year when shit hits the fan. It is the year of unending verb charts that still make me sweat and more grammar than I've learned in any English class, and the year of starting real Latin, not just textbooks. And when I returned to Mrs. Campbell's class as a sophomore, I was a different kind of mess. High school was *hard*. I no longer got effortless As, and I had more homework than a social life. This was all compounded by my yet undiagnosed ADHD; there is a unique frustration to struggling and not knowing why, or even that, you're having such a hard time.

I still loved it, but I knew things were about to get hard, and I didn't necessarily want to try in Latin anymore. Mrs. Campbell was never going to let me get away with that.

She pushed me. I became subject to the spritz bottle attacks when I was caught off task in class, and I learned to either put my phone away or develop a better duck reflex; eventually, I took up knitting so that I could stay focused and fidget, which Mrs. Campbell encouraged because it helped me pay attention and she wanted a scarf. I came in for study sessions before the state convention (a thing high school Latin nerds do to socialize, to compensate for the Romans all being dead), and I ended up placing on several of the exams. I even did homework sometimes! I excelled at many things only because Mrs. Campbell made me.

Beyond prodding me into making an effort, she was the only teacher I really felt close with for most of high school. I skipped assemblies and the cafeteria in her classroom, and I could always chat with her about her sparkly Doc Martens or our opinions on various Doctor Who seasons. She overheard me venting to a friend about drama regarding a girl who liked me, and stepped in to offer advice or possibly a shield. Her classroom is the only place in my school that I've ever really felt at home.

What I am most thankful for is another instance of well-placed nagging, though. In eleventh grade, I learned about Virginia Governor's Latin Academy, a very competitive program where high school students spend three weeks on a college campus, no phones or access to the outside world, at Latin summer school. I skipped the interest meeting, seeing as I planned to spend my summer pirating X-Men movies and eating garlic bread, not learning classics with strangers. Mrs. Campbell hunted me down.

She accosted me after class with the application packet already printed out, and told me I had to apply. If I got in, I didn't necessarily have to go, she added when she saw my reluctance, but I had to apply.

After several classes of her harassing me to do the paperwork, I relented. I'd apply (and if my ego spoke the truth, I'd probably get in, too), and then I would *not* go, because I was certainly not enough of a nerd to spend my summer doing even more school. But why not.

Spoiler: I did go.

Latin Academy was the best experience of my life. I was suddenly surrounded with the biggest Latin nerds from dozens of classes, people like me. I disliked regular school because seventy-five percent of the classes felt meaningless, and I wished I could just study Latin, but here, *everything* was classics. In Ancient Greek, I felt that same thrill as in early Latin of learning a new language, but at a quick pace to match mine; Greek took much more work, but I loved it, because I could see my efforts turning into skills in real time. I felt a glow of pride in art history classes when we studied a scene I had translated in Mrs. Campbell's class, and I took extra notes to tell her about later.

Everything I did at Latin Academy was influenced by Mrs. Campbell. For Roman dress events, I wore the stola I'd sewn for a project the year before and a shawl I'd bought on the school trip to Italy—much classier than a bedsheet toga. I struggled initially in my spoken Latin class, but I never forgot the simple introduction framework I'd learned on my very first day of Latin I, and I improved rapidly once I made myself work for it. I was always shocked when my new friends expressed neutrality or even dislike of their own Latin teachers, because I credit Mrs. Campbell with every step that got me to Academy. She taught me almost everything I knew about Latin up until then, wrote my recommendation letter, and I would have never considered applying if not for her.

When I got back from Latin Academy, I wanted to go back to school, but only for Latin class. To make up for the sudden void in learning, I checked out every library book I could find on Ancient Greece and Rome, dove down Wikipedia rabbit holes to admire Hellenistic art, waited three agonizing weeks for my Greek textbook to ship, and longed to be taught again.

Before that summer, I had dreams of becoming a hotshot *Washington Post* reporter, and then probably the president, but the idea of political science felt distant and disappointing now. I found myself researching colleges with strong Classics programs, and tentatively, I started to tell people that I wanted to become a high school Latin teacher.

I'd always hated high school, yet always loved Latin; it was a lot of what made school tolerable for me. When I'd (very briefly) considered a teaching career before, I'd laughed the idea off, certain that I could never be happy with that much stress, that many teenagers, that little pay. Yet I'd had many Latin teachers who seemed genuinely happy with their jobs, stressful as they were, and these teachers all loved me like few others had.

I loved Latin, I was good at Latin, and I had an endless capacity for explaining things, so maybe it could work. And my Latin teachers have changed the way I saw learning, the way I saw language, and even the way I saw myself; no one has affected me as strongly as this group of people. All I wanted in life, I realized, was to be the kind of person that Mrs. Campbell and my other Latin teachers are, and there was a pretty clear route for me.

I returned to Mrs. Campbell's class in the fall as a changed student, a good one who she rarely had to prod to make an effort. I turned in my homework every class, since I'd promised a Latin Academy teacher that I'd be more diligent about it now; I endured a spritz bottle attack and feigned outrage for mentioning that to Mrs. Campbell, since I'd ignored her pleas to do my work for a while before that, but at least I was doing it now. At the beginning of the year, she'd regularly accuse me of being on my phone like I'd so often been in the past, but I was innocent every time. I think I surprised us both with how much I'd improved.

My initial confession that I may want to teach Latin escalated into her joking fodder every time I complained; "It's just a weird verb form! And you say you want to be a Latin teacher!" "Oh, stop complaining and do the essay! Don't you want to be a Latin teacher!" "You want to be a Latin teacher! Just translate the lines!" Every class I became more and more certain that this is what I wanted to do with my life.

I began eighth grade slightly intimidated by the loud, enthusiastic teacher who was really excited about those Romans, and now as a high school senior, I don't know what I'd do without her. When I try to imagine who I'd be if I hadn't chosen Latin, the concept is incomprehensible, because it's become so enmeshed with my identity. My skill at Latin was my rock in a stormy eighth grade, and my Latin teacher was the one who kept me pushing on when I got frustrated and wanted to give up in high school. I spent half a summer voluntarily sacrificing technology and free time to learn about Ancient Rome, and I loved it so much that I kept learning once I had to leave, and I haven't stopped learning since; I never want to stop learning now.

Mrs. Campbell has put up with me for five years, which is commendable by any means, because I can be a lot to put up with that. But more than that, she's made me better; she was one of the few teachers bold enough to tell me to try harder, and I doubt I ever would have tried without her to give me the push. She won't let me get away with anything remotely near a lapse in effort and keeps me grounded when I begin to feel too important for the homework, and I appreciate and need that more than I'm sometimes willing to admit. She has supported and pushed me at once, and she is the reason I'm moving upward.

MEGAN SULLIVAN IS A SOMEWHAT PRETENTIOUS EIGHTEEN-YEAR-OLD CLASSICIST LIVING IN THE WASHINGTON, DC AREA, CURRENT HIGH SCHOOL LATIN STUDENT, AND ASPIRING HIGH SCHOOL LATIN TEACHER. SHE HAS PREVIOUSLY BEEN PUBLISHED IN *YOU DO YOU*. IF ANY OF HER OTHER LATIN TEACHERS ARE READING THIS, SHE'S SORRY YOU ONLY GOT CAMEOS BUT WANTS YOU TO KNOW THAT SHE COULD FILL A BOOK OR MORE WITH HER GRATITUDE TOWARD YOU, ET GRATIAS OMNIBUS.

3

Home is the School Where the Navy Sends Us
By Erin Rovak Henderschedt

I 'm a military spouse: Commander in Chief at Home and mom to four sons, but my first children were teenagers, and I was only twenty-four years old at the time; that's because I'm also a teacher.

My inaugural class was a rowdy group of thirty kids from a rough suburb of Glasgow, Scotland, and in typical student fashion, they frequently (accidentally) called me "Mom." It was harmless and happened ALL. THE. TIME. As teachers, we spend a tremendous amount of time with our students, often racking up more "face time" hours than that of their own family members. Teachers are, therefore, the most significant, unrelated presence in children's lives.

For our family, home is where the US Navy sends us, and schools are perhaps the most important part of each place we settle. The house, neighbors, and amenities are not insignificant, but my kids' teachers always prove to be one of the most important factors in making a move successful. Teachers can make or break the transition to a new locale for all of us. We've been blessed because to present day, we've never had a teacher mess that up. Sure, immediate family and friends are important wherever we go, but extended family is usually hundreds, if not thousands, of miles away. Teachers spend over seven hours a day, five days a week, with our kids, and their ability to truly see my children and anticipate their emotional needs is a tremendous gift. A teacher is a guiding figure, a role model and a confidant. Their integral role in our kids' social and emotional well-being cannot be overstated.

I, too, depend on teachers to help ease my entrée into a new community. Schools are micro communities and generally very welcoming. While my kids were young I took a long break from teaching, but work to join a school faculty as soon as I feel comfortable that my kids are settled into each new setting.

My high school English teacher prophesied that I'd be an educator well before I even considered it myself. Just before graduation, she asked everyone in our small class to predict where we'd be in ten years. I said I'd be living in a posh apartment in Washington, DC, with a high-powered political job. Mrs. N laughed and said, "No way, Rovak! You're definitely going to be a teacher, married with at least one child, maybe more, living in the suburbs." At the time, I resented the implication that I wouldn't follow my dream, but less than a year later, I realized what she was forecasting *was* my dream after all.

I began to appreciate that teaching might actually be my calling when I was a freshman in college in Washington, DC. I interned for my congressman and had the privilege of speaking to my little sister's high school civics class to share the ins and outs of what happens on Capitol Hill while I was home in Missouri over winter break. The lively interaction and instant bond I felt with the students had an immediate and dramatic impact on me. I loved sharing my knowledge and sparking interest in the young scholars. Still, I imagined I'd have a career in politics and eventually move into teaching later in life. I graduated with a B.A. in international affairs three years later and spent a few short years working in my intended field until finally it become painfully obvious that I was born to teach. I ultimately packed my bags, moved home to St. Louis, and went back to school to get certified. In a year and a half, I finished my student teaching, got married, and moved overseas for the first time.

Luckily, teaching is an occupation that is perfect for military spouses. Schools are everywhere, and they almost always need more educators. Home is where the military sends us, and I can teach wherever we are sent. We've moved 12 times in 23 years, landing in communities in Washington, DC, Scotland, Virginia (northern and southern), Hawaii, Washington state, Missouri, Kansas, China, and Taiwan, and I've taught in about half of them, ever since all of my kids were in school. Wherever I go, the story is the same, teachers are key to our kids' well-being.

Let's face it, our children's teachers often know way more about our lives than we'd prefer. At Morning Meeting sharing time, when I was teaching third grade for a year in Northern Virginia, young McKenzie wondered aloud why her parents needed to stay at a hotel in the same town where they live to celebrate their anniversary. As this would not be what we call "a teachable moment," I moved the conversation along to the next child who shared with heartache that his family had to give their puppy away because his dad was allergic to it. It led to a very meaningful lesson about loss.

While parenting is certainly not in the official teachers' employment manual, it is definitely part of the job. To varying degrees, it's necessary. Sometimes it's just a matter of timing. Lucky for us, teachers are present for our kids when we can't be, and I am grateful for that; and I'm grateful to be in a position to be there too.

ERIN ROVAK HENDERSCHEDT WRITES ABOUT MILITARY FAMILY ISSUES FOR VARIOUS WEBSITES, MOSTLY DEPLOYMENT DIATRIBES. SHE'S

ALSO BEEN PUBLISHED IN *REDBOOK, USA TODAY MAGAZINE*, POP SUGAR, THE STIR, AND DAILY CALLER. SHE, HER NAVAL OFFICER HUSBAND, AND FOUR SONS CURRENTLY SERVE OUR COUNTRY IN CHINA; HOME IS ST. LOUIS.

4

Dear Teachers: Here's My Kid—Weld Him, Shape Him, Love Him
By Monica Gokey

"I'm going to forest school all by myself!" my oldest bragged in the minivan.

"NOOOOO!" his younger brother other wailed.

The oldest was right. It was his first day of drop-off preschool. September. Three-and-a-half-years-old. And not just any preschool, but *forest school*. It's the all-outdoors kid kingdom that doubles as preschool in our nearby outdoorsy ski town. Sometimes I wish I could go to forest school and make pinecone crafts and leaf sun-catchers ... but alas, I'm merely the chauffeur and financier of such fun.

My oldest started singing a different tune as we pulled into the state park (aka classroom).

"I don't wanna go to forest school."

"I don't wanna go to forest school."

"I don't wanna go to forest school."

It's a familiar chorus.

We tried drop-off forest school a year ago and eventually had to throw in the towel after several weeks of picking him up midway through class. He'd been inconsolable.

A year later, I tried the same things I'd tried the year before. I launched into an upbeat refrain of, "I know you're nervous, but it's going be so much fun! You're going to love it! Look how much your little brother wants to go!"

He wasn't so easily swayed. His protests gave way to silence.

When we pulled up in front of the school's canvas-covered tent, his whole body became a tiny emoticon of sad. He became sullen, eyes glued to the ground.

I walked him over to the forest classroom, having left my other two kids in the car. When I turned to leave, his sniffles gave way to full-on wails.

"NO, MAMA! DON'T GO!!!!"

He roared. Then sobbed. His face was plastered with snot and tears.

My heart broke into a thousand tiny pieces.

"Should I leave?" I asked one of the teachers.

"It usually gets better when parents leave," she said kindly.

So I turned and went back to the van. His screaming echoed in my ears.

This is what heartless parents do, I told myself. *This is cruel.*

I peeled out of the parking lot and left him behind anyway.

OUTSIDE A DIFFERENT PARKING LOT, months later, a woman stopped me and said, "I know you."

My husband and I were enjoying a rare Sunday morning to ourselves. We went to brunch and had just checked out at the small grocery store in our rural Idaho town of 900 when the woman stopped me.

I stared back at her blankly.

"You were one of my students," she said. Her face was dead serious, like she was staring down a probable Crime Stoppers suspect.

I politely chuckled and told her I'd married into Idaho, that I wasn't originally from here.

"I'm not from Idaho either," she said.

Her insistence *did* reflect a familiar nuttiness.

"I'm from northern Virginia."

As soon as she said it, I knew exactly who was looking at me.

"DEMBY!?"

Demby had been a fixture in my life for all four years of high school. She was the school's lacrosse coach and freshman biology teacher. The fact that she was here, stopping me on my way out of our small-town grocery store, was mind-boggling.

She laughed and asked if I'd taken her for a crazy old lady.

I grinned and told her I had.

We caught up briefly by the checkout line and then exchanged phone numbers.

That night I couldn't stop thinking about Demby. Seeing her dredged up so many memories from high school.

As our lacrosse coach, I remembered her punishing long-distance runs. Before ninth grade I'd never run more than a mile—and even then, I'd only ever run a mile as a mandatory component of PE class (it was something I'd done grudgingly, not to mention slowly). From the first day of lacrosse practice in the spring and then throughout the season, Demby had us running three to four miles *before* practice. I was crippled after the first day. I could barely walk up the stairs at school the following morning, and somehow I did it all over again at practice that afternoon—the run, then practice. And then again the next day too.

As the freshman biology teacher, I have a vivid memory of Demby teaching sex ed. She had this box at the front of the classroom that students could use to ask questions anonymously. One day she pulled out a question: "Does it hurt to get semen in your eye?" The class was on the verge of erupting. Demby stayed cool. She was like a flight attendant with her hand gestures toward the eye, and like a David

Attenborough narrating that, indeed, any foreign matter to the eye can be an irritant.

As a coach, Demby was hard. But it was the kind of hardness that goes hand in hand with caring about how kids turn out. I was on junior varsity my freshman year. One day at practice she pulled me up to scrimmage with varsity when they were short a few players. One play, a defender hucked the ball downfield from goal. Everyone hurtled for the catch. It was a total Hail Mary. My defender and I sprinted madly forward, sticks out. I had the end of my stick in one hand, feebly reaching forward as far as I could. With a final lunge, the ball miraculously landed in my net. It was hard to tell who was more surprised—me, or everyone who'd seen the catch.

What wasn't surprising, to Demby at least, was that I'd outrun my defender by strides to make it to the ball. I was as fast and fit as I'd ever been, and it showed.

∿

THAT FIRST DAY at forest school, my oldest had a *hard* day. As a way to help him identify his feelings, his teachers helped him write notes to his family members through all the tears.

To his little sister: *I hope you come back.*

To his little brother: *I miss you.*

To his dad: *I miss you Dad. I wish I could stay home with you.*

And to me, his mom: *You're at the store and I feel frustrated.*

We felt so fortunate that his teachers are such saintly people. A number of teachers would've called for pickup after the first hour of crying. (Realistically, maybe after twenty minutes.)

But three hours later at pickup, a glimmer of hope: "I went to forest school all by myself," he said proudly.

Should we keep going? My husband and I talked about it for hours out of his earshot. We invested in books with titles like, "The Highly Sensitive Child" and "Children: The Challenge."

We phoned a friend for advice (also the founder of the school), to get the honest take on whether our kid's hurdles were detracting from the rest of the class, and whether he was ready. She insisted there was no reason for kids to be in school at three-and-a-half—that we shouldn't feel bad *at all* if it didn't work out. She also said the transition usually gets better each class.

So we persisted.

At three-and-a-half, we reasoned, drop-off preschool is a doable developmental milestone.

All our reasoning made sense—but in practice, it felt cruel. Each of those early weeks was a battle. My son would wake up as early as six, sulking as soon as he knew it was a forest school day. He'd start protesting an hour or more before we even started the car.

When we finally got to class, approaching the climax of this whole event—the dreaded drop-off—his sad silence and eventual sobbing cut straight through me. To say I felt like a bad parent is too crass to cover the range of self-hatred I felt in those early weeks.

This kind of moment is emblematic of the hardest thing about being a parent, knowing when to rely on reason versus instinct. My instincts were running hot with mixed messages. *He can do this. He'll get there* ... versus ... *This is traumatic. We should stop.*

As his parents, we felt we had a trade-off: We could do this now—do this drop-off thing like we were ripping off a Band-Aid—or we could wait until our oldest entered kindergarten. The latter sounds attractive in a lot of ways, but our local public school is a question mark for us. About half our school district homeschools, and most of what I know about the school is what I read in the newspaper and hear from other parents: that middle-grade reading comprehension is so low the school got an emergency infusion of cash from the state; that a teacher quit unexpectedly during the school year; that our friends who are teachers there send their kids to a more affluent school district to the north. The public school is a big, murky unknown we'll have to venture into when the time comes. But for now, I *knew* forest school. And I loved everything about it, especially the teachers.

Our son's two teachers are kind, gentle souls. They're the kind of teachers who offer nose wipes and check for dry mittens, who keep the class rich in hugs and high fives. They're the kind of people my husband and I have as friends. And when we looked at it that way, we couldn't think of anyone better to usher our oldest through his tough transition to drop-off preschool.

AFTER OUR MIRACULOUS reunion at the grocery store, Demby and I met up for a cross-country ski before she headed home to Virginia.

Our roles were reversed: I was the one picking her up in my truck, showing her how to push and glide on skinny skis, and asking if she was warm enough. (She was sweating profusely, which gave me small pleasure to the tune of, "take that," as I mentally ticked through the lacrosse drills I did for years on hot summer afternoons.)

We skied for two hours and talked about everything under the sun—the challenges of caring for (and relating to) aging parents, of being underappreciated at work, of watching our kids fail and muddle their way through adolescence.

We also talked about new things, things Demby sees in schools, and things I hear about from my peers: helicopter parenting, the insane pressure on students in the run-up to college admissions, and the achievement-driven culture of my old high school.

Demby told me about her current team. She coaches field hockey now. Nobody calls her "Demby" anymore. They call her "Coach B." At a time where kids err on the side of casual, Demby insists on the professional distance.

She told me about her son, who's playing Division I football, and what the recruitment process was like. It was a long road—literally, they traveled everywhere—to find the best fit for him. They saw football programs where male chauvinism was uncomfortably high, and programs where coaches took the hard-assed approach to conditioning (heat exhaustion, be damned!). They settled on a program that valued character and hard work. The way she talked about the program, I got the sense it's the kind of ship Demby would run if she ever set her mind to coaching Division I football.

I told her about my own parenting dramas—concern about our public school, how attached our kids are to home, and how, in general, we really like being able to raise our family in a rural setting.

It'd be fair to say that after nearly twenty years, Demby and I didn't know each other at all, and yet we also knew each other intimately. My four years of high school was a mere blip in Demby's multi-decade career as a coach and teacher (and later, administrator). But four years was enough to influence the trajectory of my life.

Reflecting on high school lacrosse under Demby's watch left me with a promising kernel of thought: Maybe the school part of school doesn't matter that much. Maybe what matters more is the people you meet along the way, the people who influence your character—people like teachers, friends, and teammates. For me, I know there were slow lessons absorbed, footstep by footstep, running the grueling pre-practice run before enduring another hour of scrimmage on shaky legs. I may not remember the phases of mitosis, but I remember when Demby ooh'd and ahh'd over my 3-D cell model in biology class. Praise never came free from Demby, and it meant so much more because of that.

Maybe great teachers aren't great because they're masters of their subject matter. Maybe they're great because of how they make us feel, and what those feelings lead us to learn about ourselves.

IT TOOK NEARLY six weeks before my son had his first no-tears drop-off.

It had been a heart-wrenching process—turning my back to his wails each morning, knowing he'd devolve into choke-sobs after I pulled away. But it had the desired effect. His self-confidence blossomed in his newfound competence at being away from his family for a half-day. Little by little, his teachers told us he cried less and less each week (with the occasional regression).

These days, he's slow to mosey back to the minivan after forest school lets out. He talks about his school friends at home, and he teaches his siblings and me how to play his favorite games and sing his favorite songs from preschool.

His two teachers are the ones we can thank (profusely) for his turnaround. Their work goes above and beyond what they're paid. (Having seen their jobs advertised, I can say this with confidence.) Their attitude and mannerisms are rubbing off in all the right ways. For example, my son will sometimes say, "You get what you get and you don't throw a fit!" when he's served food he doesn't care for. This brilliant line didn't come from us, but we employ it with gusto at family meals.

Sending your kids to school is an uncomfortable truce. What you're really doing is sending them out into the world to be shaped by extra-family forces entirely out of your control—some good, some bad. Teachers are the angels we trust to make that time positive.

My son had the predictable experience of returning home with less than desirable behaviors—he somehow learned to roar within inches of his brother's face, teeth bared, to intimidate him (it works). But he's also learned *incredible* things I'm embarrassed I hadn't thought to teach him this early, like how to wipe the table and sweep the floors after meals, and why he needs to wash his hands before handling other people's food. (He also learned things of a more basic nature ... like how to count to sixteen.)

Preschool is teaching him to be himself in the world.

Whenever I see him walking back to the minivan after forest school lets out, my son always seems light years older to me. He glows. He can rattle off what they did, what they played, and what they had for snack. He's growing in ways I never would've anticipated, and it's largely because of such a positive school culture, not to mention his teachers and their bottomless supply of patience and kindness.

AFTER SEEING Demby at our local grocery store, nearly twenty years after high school, I spun out on a daydream of my oldest someday running into his preschool teachers in the lift line somewhere—maybe in another ski town, maybe the one forest school is in.

Maybe they'll recognize each other and catch the same chairlift.

Maybe they'll laugh about forest school, about the colossal amount of snot a thirty-six-pound body can generate when it misses its parents.

Maybe my son will gain some perspective on how hard teaching is —how his teachers knew him and his classmates so well they could tell whose black snow bibs were whose, and who was going to need to hop on the snack train before a serious meltdown.

I hope my son—all my kids, for that matter—will someday understand just how many people helped shape their character over the years. His parents, after all, could only do so much. It was inevitable (and entirely healthy) that he go out into the world and learn things on his own. What his parents could do, he'll hopefully realize, was to make a delicate choice on which teachers would steward his hardest early childhood transition... the first time he left the nest.

MONICA GOKEY IS A PRINT AND RADIO JOURNALIST IN WEST-CENTRAL IDAHO. HER WORK HAS AIRED ON PUBLIC RADIO STATIONS ACROSS THE WEST AND ALASKA. SHE WRITES ABOUT THE OUTDOORS, PARENTING, AND AGRICULTURE FROM HOME ON A CATTLE RANCH, WHERE KIDS AND COWS ARE HER MOST FREQUENT INTERRUPTIONS. YOU CAN FIND HER ON TWITTER @MAGOKEY, AND ONLINE AT MONICAGOKEY.COM.

5
_____

The Kids I'm Here to Teach
By Julianna Miner

I teach public health at a local university with an almost embarrassing nerdlike fervor. If you get me started on multi-drug resistant gonorrhea or flu pandemics, I may not realize that your eyes have glazed over. I will keep talking until you pretend you have an urgent appointment and walk quickly away from me. Not everyone gets as excited as I do about these things, and I've come to accept that.

My love of public health is only part of why I teach, though. I mostly do it because I love the students. I'm not just talking about the kids I teach, I'm talking about all of them. Young people today are great and largely misunderstood. I see so many articles bemoaning their shortcomings and handwringing about the future. Some people call them the "selfie generation," which I find to be rude and self-serving. Some call them Generation Z, because they come after millennials, or iGen, because they're so defined by their relationship to technology.

I think they're remarkable, for a million reasons. Sometimes between classes, I'll sit on a bench and watch them all go about their day. Many of them walk through campus, and perhaps their lives, appearing to be checked out. Maybe they're staring at their phones or so immersed in whatever their large and expensive headphones are playing that the rest of the world seems not to exist. Or maybe it's a tactic to decompress between classes or to be alone with their thoughts for a few minutes.

Others seem acutely (painfully?) aware of everything and everyone around them. It should almost be labeled a condition: Acute Situational Awareness. I don't have it, but I imagine it's both a blessing a curse, like being able to hear other people's thoughts. I see those kids and think, that's got to be hard.

Then there are all the others who walk by me, somewhere in between those who appear to be seeing everything or almost nothing.

I see boys that are desperate for someone to take a chance on them. My heart swells for them and I hope that very soon, someone will. I hope whoever that person is, that they'll be kind and funny, and like the same kind of movies and takeout places.

I see other boys, ones who sail across the commons, looking certain that if they asked for a chance, they'd get it. Lord, we all know those boys, and we all know they'll definitely get it. I see some who are really just large, adorable children. And I see young men with the realization of what adulthood means for them written on their faces.

I see confident, pretty girls—sure, the whole world is watching them. They're right, too. Everyone is watching them. I sigh and admire them, pausing to wonder how they'll feel at my age when the admiration will be invariably diminished. Will it be a relief? Will it be a great sadness?

I watch the girls I used to be: shoulders slumped, sucking on a cigarette (who am I kidding—they all vape now), and hoping no one can tell how messed up they feel. I see painfully self-conscious girls praying they're invisible but also sad to be unnoticed.

I see so many of the students looking hesitant. Faces that seem to convey: "I don't belong here. How long till everyone else figures out that I shouldn't be here?" I know that look because I see it in the mirror. I saw it when I was their age and on a bad day, I see it now. Imposter Syndrome starts young and always outstays its welcome.

It kills me to see them doubt themselves. I know what they're capable of because I teach them every semester. They are insightful and creative. They work hard and solve problems. The push through a level of distraction and noise that fights for their attention every moment, something I simply couldn't have done at their age.

Every once in a while, I see young women striding across campus just doing their thing. Sometimes alone and sometimes with friends. Smiling, looking around, *seeing things*. Focused on where they're going and actively not giving a shit who might be watching. I am so impressed by these girls.

Their world is so different from the one I inhabited at their age and I don't think this new one is easier to navigate. I think it's simultaneously limitless and also 4 inches tall. I think it creates impossible expectations and is full of unseen consequences. I think they're inescapably aware of risks, threats, and uncertainties in a way no prior generation has been, having come of age under a cloud of mass shootings and terrorism, knowing no other reality. Yet statistically, they're more safe. Their world is full of dichotomies, ones the adults (with our fully formed frontal lobes and smugly earned life experience) struggle to make sense of. To be confronted with all this (along with all the other trappings of adolescence and early adulthood that more than challenged me) and to see them striding across campus with their heads high ... I'm in awe of them.

They are half my age and they are my role models. The sight of them strengthens me and makes me feel brave. The knowledge that so many of them are out there, ready to step into the world makes me so happy I could squeak. I could be more like that, I think to myself. Even better, my daughters could be like that. *Oh God, I pray my daughters are like that.*

These girls would never apologize for being smart. They would never stay quiet if they knew the answer. They would go for it even if it might not work out. They certainly wouldn't walk away from something BIG because someone else might not like it. They would listen to their gut, but not let their fear stop them. If someone sneered at them or their success, I think they'd shrug and walk on.

The same is true for the boys. There are ones who shine brightest, who walk tall, making eye contact and talking to everyone. The ones who always seem to show courtesy and respect, to those walking near them by the student center, and to those who disagree with them in class. Good guys are out there in larger numbers than the world and the internet would have us believe, and they give me hope.

These kids are special. They're standing at the start of their lives with so much potential and so much confidence, and it's just beautiful to see. For these kids, I'm here to teach them about public health, write their recommendations, and cheer them on as they take flight. That's my privilege, but that's not why I teach.

It's all the other students, the ones who have moments where they honestly don't know what the hell is going on or what they're going to do next, they're the real reason I'm here. These are the kids who haven't yet figured out how much potential they have. The ones who wonder if they really deserve to be there. These are my people.

I remember very clearly being a young person who was my own worst enemy, and perhaps it takes one to know one. Maybe it just takes one to have empathy for one, I don't know. Every semester there is someone in one of my sections who is a master at getting in their own way and making their life harder than it needs to be. Sometimes I find out more about them, sometimes I don't. Sometimes I'm given the opportunity to step in and work with them, but often I'm not.

In my mind, I take them by the shoulders and say, "There's nothing wrong with you, kid. We're all faking it. YES, EVEN ME. You're doing great! You have everything you need to make it in this world and you deserve it all. Go get it! What are you waiting for?! Don't be afraid!" Then I deliver a baseball-style ass smack as they nod at me knowingly and briskly jog off to conquer new territory or apply to grad school. But I never actually do that because in real life it would be weird and also extremely inappropriate.

So instead I try to be the kind of teacher I needed. I ask them to talk to me and make myself available. I probably accommodate students who ask for help a little too much, which generally makes my job harder. Because sometimes, even with empathy and extensions and extra help, they still bail on you and on themselves.

Even when that happens, I may grumble, but I don't regret trying. I know how hard these kids are working and I see what they're dealing with. The world is an infinitely smaller, more complicated, and less hopeful place than it has ever been. Everywhere they look they see the evidence of it. Yet they get up every day and do the best they can, and yes sometimes they fail. But failure is a better teacher than I will ever be, so I remind of that and encourage them to find the lesson in it. I tell them the day they make the choice to work through the hard stuff that feels overwhelming, instead of curling into a ball of bad choices and feeling like garbage about them, is the day their real life starts.

If they learn nothing else in college, they've gotten a good education.

JULIANNA W. MINER IS AN ADJUNCT PROFESSOR OF PUBLIC HEALTH AT A UNIVERSITY SHE COULDN'T HAVE GOTTEN INTO BECAUSE SHE MADE BAD CHOICES IN HIGH SCHOOL. SHE'S THE AUTHOR OF *RAISING A SCREEN SMART KID: EMBRACE THE GOOD AND AVOID THE BAD IN THE DIGITAL AGE.* SHE'S ALSO A CONTRIBUTING AUTHOR OF THE *NEW YORK TIMES* BESTSELLER *I JUST WANT TO PEE ALONE* AND OF THE AWARD-WINNING HUMOR BLOG *RANTS FROM MOMMYLAND.* HER WORK HAS BEEN FEATURED IN *THE WASHINGTON POST, PARENTS MAGAZINE, THE TODAY SHOW, THE HUFFINGTON POST, COSMO.COM,* AND MANY OTHERS. SHE LIVES IN SUBURBAN WASHINGTON, DC, WITH HER THREE KIDS, TWO DOGS, AND ONE HUSBAND.

6

"What is F*****"
By Alexandra Rosas

I t had been a long week in the classroom. The kind of week where teachers should be paid in diamonds, rubies, pearls, because money was just trifling with the amount of exertion the last four days had cost. At lunch duty, there had been a bloody nose. During an art project, some kids decided they liked the blue paint better on their palms than on the paper in front of them, and then when it was time for the class to walk together for an all school assembly, two students decided that was the time they wanted to go to the nurse's office.

That afternoon, there was even more fun coming my way. It was the week to give out sola system and planet assignments. Any teacher out there will know what I'm talking. Ever have to say, "Time to assign Uranus," to a group of elementary school kids? Let me tell you, you haven't lived until you've said, "I need a group of four for Uranus." Try it sometime; the classroom response will give you nightmares for day.

But here we are, finally at Thursday afternoon. We were almost to the finish line for the week.

I dismissed the class and the kids physically readied their backpacks and notebooks. I mentally readied my own going-home arsenal. My first stop without a doubt would be a splurge. Usually reserved for Friday nights, there was a ready to go pizza place on my way home. Well, not exactly on the way home, but I could still find my way home from the twenty minutes there and twenty minutes back. What's the harm in starting Friday a day early? Soon, the week would be over, hell, I'd even pick up a quart of root beer for my teen son despite his three not five-star cleaning at his orthodontist checkup last week. Like I said, it had been a hell of a long week.

I was collecting my papers to head on out when I first heard the rumble in the hallway.

"Ooooh! She said it! She said it!"

"You're in so much trouble!"

"Teacher! She said a bad word!"

I sighed and stepped into the hall. On one side, I see fingers pointing. I hear shouts, accusations, gasps.

On the other side, I see her. Eyes down on the ground, the fingers of her hands twisting together.

"She said it! She said it!" The kids were voices upon voices now. "We all heard her!"

I stood in between both groups. "Quiet now, please! Get your things ready! I'll take care of this!" The kids began to grab their things and quickly the talk turned to what video game they'd play as soon as they got home. They began to pair up for the walk home, for bus partners, for carpools.

I walked over to her, she was quiet, frightened. "What did you say? Why don't you tell me what the kids are talking about?" I pushed her dark hair away from her forehead.

"She said the bad word! We heard it!" A few stragglers insisted on being heard.

"I'm asking her, not you, aren't I? Now home, please!" I looked back at her now and asked again. There was only more silence.

The kids scattered, their voices fading. The echo of the once full hall falling away.

When we were together in silence, I knelt down. "Hey, I want to tell you something," I had to get down to eye level. "When I was in your grade, just like you are now, this very same thing happened to me. About the bad word."

I see her brown eyes flicker up. "To you?"

"Yes. My family was new to this country. And one day in class, I said a bad word. I didn't know what it meant. I said it because I had heard it, and my teacher then was Miss Quill. She was sitting at her desk in the front of the room, and out of nowhere, all the kids in class went running up to her desk, saying that I had said a bad word. I was scared, I didn't know what they were talking about. I had heard someone say something, so I said it, and now I was in trouble for the same thing someone else had just done. And I didn't even know what it was. No one would ever purposely say a bad word in school, right?" I could almost hear her heart beating as she listened.

"Then what happened?" she asked. "Did you get in trouble?"

"Well, Miss Quill took me into the hall and talked to me. She asked me what happened, and I told her."

Three beats of silence, then, "Teacher?"

"Yes?"

"I didn't know it was a bad word, Teacher." Her voice was tight. "I wouldn't say a bad word."

"I believe you. And I believe you won't say it again either, because you didn't know before, but you know now. Just like after I knew, I never said it again. So, we both know now, that's not a word we'll ever say."

She stood, toes pointed in, her hands tight against her sides. "Will you have to tell my dad when he comes?"

"Yes, I will." I sighed, there was no way to soften the blow of bad news. "But only because Miss Quill told my mother. So that my mother would help me remember to not say it again."

"But I don't want you to tell my dad!" Now her tears of frustration, long held back, flooded.

"I'll tell him about me first, all right? About me, when I was little and I said the bad word. And then I'll tell him about today. He'll listen. We'll tell him together. Come on now, let's get ready. School's out!"

With eyes down, she slowly gathered her things. We walked together down the hall to the main door, where her family would be waiting.

"Teacher? What did they call you when you were little?"

"You mean my name? It was Alex."

"That's my brother's name!" Finally, a lilt to her voice.

"My name was Alex. And now that you know that, guess what?"

"What?"

"You can keep calling me Teacher."

She covered her mouth, laughing in surprise. Her eyes twinkled with relief at feeling better. After a few seconds, she asked shyly, "Are you from Ecuador too?"

Now I was the one surprised with her specific question. "No. I'm not. Why do you ask?"

"You're like me. Your name, and how you just moved here, and said a bad word and didn't know."

"No, I'm not from Ecuador, but my family comes from a different country. And like you, I was just learning English too. That's why I didn't know the bad word—I was just saying something I heard. That's how you didn't know the bad word either. And Miss Quill somehow knew that about me too."

"You're like the Miss Quill today, right? You're the one who knows I didn't know."

My eyes began to blur, stunned by the moment. Yes, I was now my wonderful teacher from so long ago, Miss Quill. "I guess so," I answered. "Yes, in a way, I am Miss Quill. And I'll always remember how she understood how different things were for me than for the other children who came from this country."

Up ahead, we see her father waiting with her little brother, Alex. I handed her backpack to her father, and explained the day. As I promised, I began with my story. And Miss Quill, and the bad words, from both his daughter, and me, once upon a time.

We finished, everything ending with polite smiles. His daughter running ahead, her little brother by the hand. Her father lagged behind, staying for a minute. After a pause, he asked me, "What was the bad word she said?"

"Well." I hesitated, "It's an American word. Not a nice one. It's f*****."

His reply was identical to my mother's decades ago when she leaned in and Miss Quill told her the bad word that I had said.

"What is f*****?"

ALEXANDRA ROSAS IS A FIRST-GENERATION AMERICAN WHO HAS BEEN WRITING CULTURAL MEMOIR AND HUMOR SINCE 2006. SHE WAS CO-PRODUCER OF THE NATIONALLY ACCLAIMED LISTEN TO YOUR MOTHER SHOW, AND IS A MULTIPLE WINNER OF THE BLOGHER VOICE OF THE YEAR AWARD FOR HUMOR. ALEXANDRA HAS TOLD STORIES FOR THE MOTH AND IS A GRANDSLAM CHAMPION OF THE MILWAUKEE AND MADISON SHOWS. SHE HAS BEEN PUBLISHED IN VARIOUS HUMOR AND WRITING SITES, INCLUDING SCARY MOMMY, *THE HUFFINGTON POST*, AND GROWN AND FLOWN. AWARDED THE NATIONAL GOLD AND SILVER PARENTING MEDIA AWARD FOR HER WRITING, SHE CONTINUES TO CONTRIBUTE ON PARENTING TEENS.

7

Mrs. Norton's Daughter
By Nicole Norton Mueller

M y mother graduated college in 1978 and moved 230 miles south of her hometown for her first teaching job. She'd accepted a position as a Title I reading teacher for a countywide elementary school. The entire building serviced about five hundred K-5 students. But she wasn't going to be teaching IN the building. She was going to be teaching in a trailer. Next to the building. In the parking lot.

The story is that her father made the drive down to make sure she was settled into her new apartment and asked to see the school. He soon realized his daughter was going to be spending her workday crammed into a beige tin can with two other teachers. She didn't have her own classroom or an office. In fact, the trailer was divided into thirds by partial walls, so she didn't even have the luxury of silence during her prep period.

After taking all this in, my grandfather looked her in the eye and said: "You don't HAVE to do this, you know. You can come home with me. Right. Now."

But she DID do it. Soon enough she was moved to working inside the actual building, got married, and got promoted to a position as a third-grade teacher. Mrs. Norton was "born."

A few years later, I was born too. In a town of about twenty-six hundred people. In a town where everybody knows everybody. In a town where I spent many years being known solely as "Mrs. Norton's daughter."

This is the story of my survival.

Okay, okay. Maybe "survival" is a little dramatic. But the older I get, the more I realize that I didn't have a typical childhood educational experience.

For starters, my mother handpicked all of my classroom teachers from kindergarten through fourth grade. To give her credit, she always pretended to be surprised when the class lists were announced each year. ("*Oh! You got Mrs. Brown! She's super nice. You're going to learn so much!*") There also always seemed to be this slightly odd relationship between the adults on staff in the building and me. They all knew my name because most of them had known my mother for years. This seemed to result in me getting called on more than the other kids, especially during the first few weeks of a new school year when the teachers were still trying to remember everyone's names.

I was often the first kid picked to be the "student of the week," the first kid picked to bring an item for "show and tell," or the first kid picked to read out loud to the class. When I was little, being called out for these things just made me feel special. As I got older? Let's just say I didn't appreciate the entire art class staring at my mouth while we were supposed to be learning how to draw lips.

The atypical relationship I had with my mother's coworkers also extended to discipline. Unbeknownst to my mother, I can remember running in the halls after school using my "outside voice." I have clear memories of some teachers angrily poking their heads out of their classrooms, realizing it was me, and then just laughing and going about their business. But the opposite was also true. I once got a lengthy lecture from a fifth-grade teacher when she found me messing around in a bathroom after school. (Apparently it's frowned upon to turn all five water faucets on at once when you're washing your hands.)

I'd like to say that all the awkwardness was contained within the elementary school building, but that would be a lie. Local shopping with my mother was almost guaranteed to result in some random kids staring at you in public because they didn't realize that Mrs. Norton even EXISTED outside of the classroom. But I'd prefer the gawking over the uncomfortable exchanges. Doesn't everyone want to have a forced conversation with an eight-year-old while your mother is helping you peruse the "feminine product" aisle for the first time? Mortifying.

And like it or not, my mother's reputation at school affected mine. I wouldn't go as far as to say she was mean to her students, but she definitely didn't tolerate any BS in her classroom. This sort of left my classmates thinking that I operated the same way. In fact, I don't remember having any real friends who wanted to hang out outside of school until about fourth grade. And even then, it was problematic.

Kids would come over to my house and act, well, weird because my Mom was there. It was as if they couldn't bring themselves to relax because a TEACHER was in the next room. It didn't seem to matter that she was on the couch in her sweatpants.

It sort of felt like things went further south when I got to high school. I was in the marching band, which as geeky as it sounds, is where I started noticing older boys I wanted to date. Because I was never going to be cool enough to snag a "new kid" (those guys went like hotcakes in a school district that small), there was a one in four chance my crush was going to be one of my mother's former students. How many teenage boys do you think risked kissing me on the front step knowing their former teacher might have been looking out the window? Spoiler alert: two.

I'm sure it felt like a delicate situation for my mother also. She overhears me gushing about a cool senior boy, and all she can think about is how he used to constantly pick his nose at his desk in third grade. Or how he cried on the school field trip to the dairy farm because he was afraid of the cows. Or that she constantly had to remind him to zip his fly when he came back from the bathroom.

Perhaps being "Mrs. Norton's daughter" limited my dating prospects, but it wasn't all bad. I never experienced any of the legendary horrors of riding the school bus every day. If I happened to forget a textbook or crucial piece of homework, my mother had keys to the building so I could grab it. Even more important, I logged many hours playing Oregon Trail on the old Macintosh Classics in the school's computer lab while I waited for her to finish working. (*You have died of dysentery!*)

And now that I look back on it, I think I might have received special treatment from some of her coworkers. I don't think many of my classmates were chosen by the coach to staple and collate papers instead of running laps during gym class, or to flip through textbooks to see if they'd been defaced. Which was essentially glorified tattling. You know, I'm lucky I didn't get beat up in the sixth grade.

My mother taught in that countywide school district for thirty-seven years. Which, in case you were wondering, is long enough that she had students in her class... and then had their CHILDREN in her class as well. Talk about an awkward parent/teacher conference. ("*Well, Jordan isn't quite getting the hang of cursive yet, but you didn't master it right away either! By the way, did you ever stop eating glue?*")

While my school experiences might not have been the same as the kids who didn't run the risk of their parent waving at them across the cafeteria, I can't imagine it any other way. So thanks for not being overly embarrassing, Mom. Even if you did use "that teacher voice" on me a little too often.

NICOLE NORTON MUELLER WON AN ESSAY CONTEST (AND A SMALL CASH PRIZE) DURING HER FRESHMAN YEAR OF HIGH SCHOOL, AND HAS BEEN LOOKING FOR EXCUSES TO WRITE EVER SINCE. SHE PREVIOUSLY SERVED AS A WRITER FOR THE IOWA JOURNALIST, AND HAS CREATED MARKETING COPY FOR MULTIPLE NONPROFITS. LEARN MORE AT NICOLENORTONMUELLER.COM.

8

Watergate 2005
By Stephanie Giese

W e aren't supposed to have favorites, but some students stand out and still make you smile, just thinking of them fourteen years later. That was Davon[1]. I was a rookie fresh out of college, and he was a six-year-old who wore the same personalized Redskins Jersey every single day.

Davon loved two things: football and living life to the fullest. Our school was in an impoverished district, just outside of Washington, DC. Our students didn't have much, but Davon had his jersey. He loved football hard, more than any grown man. He memorized statistics and rules and talked constantly about the games of the week. Every day at recess he would organize a game. He was annoyed that the recess monitors made them play touch, because how was he supposed to know how to take a hit if no one would let him get tackled? He drew plays with stick figures in the margins of his papers. It was his dream to play in the NFL, and I won't be surprised if he makes it. (Truth be told, he'd be in college now and I've Googled his name a few times to see if it pops up on a team.)

I don't remember ever seeing Davon in a bad mood. He loved to tell jokes, and he was a good listener in my class, although just an average student. He didn't struggle, but he didn't excel academically either. He was steadily middle of the road, but I meant every word when I wrote on his report card that he was "a pleasure to have in class." His hand was always one of the first ones raised and if the class started to get out of hand, I could count on Davon to rein them back in.

"Hush up, she's talking!" He'd scold his classmates, then wink at me. They listened every time. His classmates worshipped him. He was the Pied Piper of first grade, and because he liked me, he used his powers for good. I can't count how many times I would just shake my head and smile. He had the charisma of Barack Obama, and the cool, collected nature of Pharrell Williams. Everyone fell in love with him.

Everyone except his arch nemesis—the recess monitor.

Davon lived for recess. Sure, all kids do, but this was a much more serious love affair. Remember Beatles or *Twilight* mania? That was Davon, only instead of screaming and pledging his love to Team Jacob, he worshiped the clock when it struck 12:15. Literally the only thing he wanted to do, ever, was get outside and run his plays.

Then one day they wouldn't let him. I wish I could remember why. I think a kindergartener had gotten hurt playing in their football game and as a result the first-grade boys were designated to the playground equipment for a few days instead.

Davon was not going to take this sitting down. He told me, "I don't like this, miss. I gotta do something." I suggested he write a letter and explain his reasons.

Apparently, he had other ideas.

I was sitting at my desk grading papers on my lunch break when my principal called my name over the intercom to head to his office as soon as possible. (By the way, getting called to the principal feels exactly the same even when you're an adult.) I frantically ran through the list of things this might be about.

I wasn't prepared to find several boys from my class sitting in chairs, hanging their heads. Davon sat in the middle, head held high, arms crossed.

He'd organized a union made entirely of six-year-olds, and they were on strike, fighting for their recess rights.

The principal told me what happened. He was not amused, but I was finding it hard to keep a straight face.

"Are you aware of the situation with recess and football?"

I told him I was, but I still wasn't quite sure why we were in the office.

He explained that several boys from my class had engaged in a "verbal altercation" with the recess monitor (I'm still not entirely sure what the altercation was between six-year-olds and an adult.) When they didn't get their way using their admittedly misguided words, the boys decided to take matters into their own hands. "Matters" in this case would be certain body parts. Apparently, in unison, they had all whipped out their you-know-whats and proceeded to urinate on the school. I mean, that's one way to show someone you're pissed at them, I guess.

Davon looked up at me. "You really gotta call my moms?"

I nodded, solemnly. We walked back to the classroom and I let him dial. Together we attempted to explain to his mother how he had been the ringleader of Watergate 2005.

She said she would handle it.

I said I'd do what I could as well.

He'd already been to the principal and had a phone call home. The only thing I did after that was make sure they got their football game back.

STEPHANIE GIESE IS A MOTHER OF FIVE AND THE WRITER BEHIND BINKIES AND BRIEFCASES. SHE HAS SERVED AS A PUBLIC SCHOOL TEACHER AND GIFTED SPECIALIST FOR GRADES 1-6 IN MARYLAND, PENNSYLVANIA, AND FLORIDA. HER WORK CAN BE FOUND ONLINE AND IN THE *NEW YORK TIMES* BESTSELLING ANTHOLOGY *I JUST WANT TO PEE ALONE*.

1. Name has been changed just in case a now-grown boy doesn't want his first-grade teacher publishing a story about that time he convinced everyone to pee on our school.

9

A Wagon and A Wink
By Darlene Deluca

In third grade, I was small, thin, and completely non-athletic—the scrawny girl who never got picked for a team in gym class. The kid who would spin completely around and fall down at home plate in an attempt to hit a soft ball. The girl who was picked ON during that hideous and humiliating "game" of torture called Red Rover. Yeah, no chance was I ever going to break through anyone's arms. Now, it's been a long while since I was in the third grade, but like most things traumatic, I remember it well.

I remember feeling positively giddy when it turned out I had to go to the hospital for a few days during softball season to get a little cyst removed. Yippee! No playground time for me!

But there was this one thing. This one time when the stars aligned or lady luck smiled upon me – thanks in no small part to my awesome third-grade teacher who forever holds a special place in my heart. One day, she (I'll call her Mrs. E) announced that the entire third-grade was having a jump rope competition. I am sure my eyes lit up. As an adult, this memory reminds me of the scene in the movie *A Christmas Story* when Ralphie's teacher announces a theme-writing assignment. Whoa-ho! Here was my chance!

I could jump rope. This was it—my chance to accomplish something that was somewhere near the realm of sporty, athletic. Competitive jump roping! To this day, I have no idea whose brilliant idea this was. I like to think my teacher, with her keenly observant eyes, had noticed my particular talent and set into motion the opportunity for me to have my moment in the spotlight. (My adult self now has some doubts about this theory.)

But I know that my teacher liked me, and she was a kind person, so why not?

Anyway, the date was set, and of course, the trash talk began. Who would beat whom? Who would achieve bragging rights, etc.? As the boys confidently decreed who among them had the best shot of winning, doubts crept in. Who was I kidding? Sure, I could jump rope, but how could scrawny little me compete against all these boys? It seemed unlikely.

On the day of the event, we all spread out inside the combination gym/lunchroom/auditorium. Heart pounding, I swiped sweaty palms against my shorts as the anticipation built. When the whistle blew, we jumped. And jumped. One by one, I watched my classmates fall. And I jumped some more. I was in a jump-rope zone, but I caught my teacher's eye as she stood off to the side watching. Through body language, her smile, clapping, whatever, I sensed Mrs. E's enthusiasm and encouragement. It all said *keep going, you can do this, I believe in you.* And I one-hundred percent believe that's what kept me going even when I began to get tired. Now I wasn't in it just for me. Now I wanted to win for her, too. I wanted it to be our class that walked away with those bragging rights.

And so I jumped some more. I jumped until I was exhausted and my legs shook. I remember they felt weak and rubbery as I climbed the couple of steps to the stage for the final rounds. Finally, only two of us remained. Of course it had to end up boy versus girl at the end. Me against him.

From that stage it was hard to make out individual faces, especially as I was bobbing around, jumping and jumping and jumping that rope until I was nearly dizzy. But I was able to see my teacher's face. Maybe because she stood while the kids in the audience were seated on the floor. Did she do that for me? I know I saw her nodding, smiling, as if she, too, had some skin in the game. As if she wanted this win for me. She was the driving force that compelled me to stick with it. I was determined not to quit until I became Jump Rope Queen!

I remember being tired. Tired of jumping. But this darn boy. He kept jumping, too. On and on and on. So I couldn't stop. Couldn't quit.

So I didn't. I kept looking at Mrs. E. Saw her smiling still. Saw her smile widen to a grin. Saw her nod and clap. *For me.*

She had, no doubt, witnessed me being clobbered by the tether ball on the playground or nearly choke myself on the chin-up bars. Or perhaps she'd seem my lame attempts to perform a back bend or climb the ropes dangling from the ceiling.

If I won this, could I redeem myself? Could I hold my head high during gym class?

After what seemed like hours of incessant jumping, I did it. I defeated that boy. He missed. He tripped over his rope and down he went. Bye, bye, boy.

Seconds after he did, I went down, too. Not because I tripped, but because I was done. I had won. It was over. So I just plopped down with my rope. Unfortunately, in my moment of glory, I ever-so-gracefully landed on my ankle. Seriously. After all of that, I couldn't get back up. So much for my amazing athleticism.

As I was officially declared the winner, I basked in my glory—as best I could from my position on the floor. (I'm still vaguely disappointed that I didn't receive a crown, or at least a tiara, as my prize.) When it became apparent that I actually could not get up to receive my accolades (and a blue ribbon), my amazing teacher came to my rescue. In the midst of the clapping, Mrs. E appeared in the gym with a little red wagon. Full of concern, she picked me up from the stage and gently deposited me into the red wagon.

Looking back, I probably should've been embarrassed. But I felt special. My teacher wheeled me out of the gym and down to the nurse's office. It was a very short ride, but I felt like I was in my private chariot and had an exclusive meeting with the queen. Was another teacher herding my classmates back to the room? Had she forgotten about them? No matter. Her attention was focused on me.

She waited while the nurse determined I had not sustained any serious injury. No broken bones. Just a little sprain.

When my teacher finally remembered she had a couple dozen other kids to tend to, she squeezed my hand and turned to leave. But she turned back for one last look. And when she met my eyes again, she winked at me. *That wink*. I don't know if we were sharing pride, a little bit of humor, if it was conspiratorial, but I know a connection was made.

I'd won. I'd accomplished something. But it wasn't just me. There was something energizing, spirit-boosting, confidence-building, about knowing that someone else was cheering for me. I had a fan, an ally. I doubt the other kids even remember the event. Well, that second-place loser might. But I will never forget it!

It didn't mean I was chosen first for any activity in phys ed, but it definitely elevated my self-esteem and earned me a little more respect among my peers—particularly among the boys.

Some time later, Mrs. E used the jump rope competition as an example in a class lesson. The point she made that day has always stuck with me. Everyone is good at something. I can't play volleyball, but I can jump rope. Some people can't do math, but they can write. Some people can't sing, but they can draw.

And sometimes all they need is a little encouragement to boost their confidence and let their talent shine. That day I won the jump rope competition I remember feeling encouraged. And the person responsible for that is my third-grade teacher.

· · ·

DARLENE DELUCA WRITES CONTEMPORARY ROMANCE AND WOMEN'S FICTION, AND LIKES TO EXPLORE RELATIONSHIPS—WHAT BRINGS PEOPLE TOGETHER OR KEEPS THEM APART. HER INTENT IS TO BRING TO LIFE INTERESTING CHARACTERS THAT READERS CAN RELATE TO IN REAL-LIFE SITUATIONS THAT COMBINE A LITTLE FUN, PLENTY OF DRAMA (WITH PERHAPS A TEAR OR TWO), AND BIG HELPINGS OF FRIENDSHIP, LOVE, AND SELF-DISCOVERY, AND WILL LEAVE YOU EITHER CHEERING OR SIGHING WITH A SATISFIED SMILE AS YOU TURN THE FINAL PAGE.

DARLENE HAS BEEN A READER AND WRITER SINCE CHILDHOOD. WITH A DEGREE IN JOURNALISM, SHE STARTED HER CAREER AS A NEWSPAPER REPORTER. THE KANSAS CITY AUTHOR CURRENTLY HAS SEVEN PUBLISHED NOVELS AVAILABLE IN PAPERBACK AND E-BOOK VERSIONS. SHE IS A STRONG PROPONENT OF EDUCATION AND HAS BEEN ACTIVE AS A PTA BOARD MEMBER, CLASSROOM VOLUNTEER, ROOM MOM, SOCCER MOM, TENNIS MOM, BAND MOM, AND GIRL SCOUT LEADER. AND SHE BELIEVES GOOD TEACHERS ARE MODERN-DAY HEROES.

SHE WRITES DAY OR NIGHT, WHENEVER THE WORDS/MOOD/DEAD-LINES STRIKE, AND ALMOST ALWAYS HAS A CUP OF TEA AND A BIT OF DARK CHOCOLATE NEARBY!

10

Sarcasm, Fart Jokes, and Other Reasons Why I'd Never Make It as a
Middle School Teacher
By Kim Bongiorno

This is a story about the time I thought I had received my calling in life. You see, my beloved Nana had been a teacher. With her many awkward quirks and big feet, she was the relative I related to the most. My love of books, reading, learning, and sharing the details of what I had learned with others mirrored hers. Like generations of nerds before me, I genuinely enjoyed being in school, so when I received what I believed to be a call from the universe to become a teacher like her, I decided to hop on to the same path.

After high school, I went to college to become an English teacher. I happily took all the mandatory courses, from child psychology to a variety of literature studies. Each morning, I dove out of my tiny dorm room bed for early morning classes dressed like a sun-sensitive troll who lived between the dusty stacks of an old library, and used my dateless weekends to take on even more reading. Soaking every-thing in brought me weirdly high levels of joy. Discussing novels, poetry, and strange old authors with rather unhealthy lifestyles with fellow students and professors was akin to taking multivitamins for my soul. I felt assured that I had heard that call correctly; I was on the right path.

Before I could finish my degree, I was shoved off the path of elbow patch sweaters and endless supplies of shiny apples. No longer able to afford tuition, I turned my focus to finding work simply to make ends meet. I was frustrated with this turn of events, but figured I'd find a way to teach in some other capacity. For years, I ended up in jobs that fostered my tendency to write up "how-to" manuals for fun. (I know, I know.) I found myself training other adults when managers realized I had a knack for breaking things down in a non-patronizing way for fellow employees who didn't like change (aka: all of them). I thrived in those moments. They placated me whenever my thoughts strayed back to my dream of being a teacher with my very own class-room of beautiful minds to mold.

Fast-forward a decade or so, and I've ended up becoming a profes-sional writer and a mom of two beautiful minds of my own. My eldest child's middle school teacher invited me into her classroom for a special writing exercise, giving me the opportunity to do for a day what I had once wished to do for a lifetime. I had the passing worry that it might be too bittersweet a reminder of what I missed out on, nudging me into the expensive logistical nightmare of going back to college to hop back on that old path I was knocked off years ago. Instead, it ended up being the bitch-slap I needed to ensure that I never got on that path again, for I am, in no uncertain terms, abso-lutely *not* schoolteacher material.

Turns out, that call from the universe I received as a teenager? It was a butt dial. Total wrong number. As much as I love kids, learning, and teaching, I now understand that I would have been a total embarrassment to the profession. I am a fallible, messy human being with an inflexible personality and style that doesn't mesh with the reality of teaching in a school environment. Here are just a handful of reasons why it's a good thing for students, faculty, administration, and parents that I never became a middle school teacher:

1. When kids annoy me, my default response is telling them to go away until they get far enough away from me that I'm no longer annoyed.

Apparently, this behavior is frowned upon in educational institutions? Once a child arrives at school, they are supposed to stay there, all up in your grill the entire day, no matter how annoying they get. *I know*, right? How is this a rule? Teachers must have levels of patience that are unnatural and unattainable by us mere mortals. I'm semi-convinced that they're androids, receiving their robotic patience implantations on the same day as their teaching certificates.

2. You're not supposed to swear in front of your students.

My daughter had to nudge me at least three times for muttering curse words under my breath when I visited her classroom, and I was having a lovely time that day! I didn't even know those words were coming out of me. I can't imagine being able to stop a, "Are you ****ing kidding me?" from exiting my mouth after a particularly long day/week/semester of school in response to that one punt-able kid (there's always one—don't try and deny it) stomping on my very last nerve. I've seen students get *way* out of hand in the classroom, and watched the faculty manage to get it under control without ever shouting four-letter words in a Scary Mom Voice. It's a glorious sight to behold.

3. Not all kids speak sarcasm.

I've had a dry sense of humor since around 1986, and it hasn't wavered since. Sarcastic quips and comments leap from my lips without thought, often aimed at the herds of children who use my home as a cafeteria-slash-youth center hangout. And I genuinely like these kids! My own offspring regularly translate my wiseass-ery for the masses, ensuring no one gets too offended by or scared of me. Teachers, however, speak in a clear, direct manner that cannot be misunderstood by young ears, and also have the ability to restrain their cranky inner thoughts to prevent them from becoming spoken words. These are talents I have never been able to learn, and I don't see that changing anytime soon.

4. You have to deal with the parents.

No, thank you.

5. There's a responsibility to not screw up the kids you teach.

I am a loving, well-intentioned mother of two who is under no illusions that I am not screwing up my own progeny little by little every day. But I am also committed to their overall mental health, willing to shell out whatever money required for the therapy they'll one day need to recover from damage I accidentally caused. It would be irresponsible of me to inflict myself upon a slew of new students every year for forty years—that is a *lot* of therapy, and it's simply not in my budget. It's best if I avoid the risk altogether. Meanwhile, the teachers I know are magical creatures with master plans that enrich our kids' brains and hearts, even when the kids moan and groan about the work. The kids always benefit. *Always.* How do they do it? I have no idea. Again: I am a mere mortal.

6. You can't steal the kids you like.

When I first visited my son's class, they had each written a short fictional story for me to review as part of the assignment. Each story had me on an emotional roller coaster, reading between the lines and building a psychological profile of the authors. We write what we know, so I was getting to understand these kids on a deeper level and caring so much about them they began to feel like my kids. Mine.

MINE. *I fell in maternal love with twenty-five additional children overnight.* How is this healthy? I barely managed to make it out of there without a couple extra kids under my arms and my heart intact (FYI: kidnapping your child's super-sweet classmates is "illegal" and will also make him mad at you for embarrassing him in front of his friends.) Teachers have these wonderful kids within arm's reach all year long, building true relationships, and never once toss a favorite into their briefcase for keepsies. That, my friends, is true grit.

7. You're supposed to be helpful, not brutally honest.

Don't get me wrong: I am my kids' biggest cheerleader. But I also know how well they can play. So when they come home with a bad grade on something and *wah wah* to me about it, my feedback holds no punches. If their sucky project got a bad grade because they did not do what they were capable of doing, I tell them it's their own fault for doing a lazy, crappy job. Next time they should live up to their potential and not be a Whiney Whinerton about something they can control. There is a reason they don't make stickers that say things like, "Great Job at Not Living Up to Your Potential!" "Fantastic Under-achieving!" "Super Lazy" and "Are You Kidding Me With This?" Teachers address these kinds of scenarios in much more pleasant, uplifting terms. Maybe they have access to a special thesaurus?

8. You're supposed to be the grown-up in the room.

Fart jokes are freaking hilarious. Most of the books I read for pleasure are for kids ages eight and up. Responsibility is poop. Shiny things easily distract me. Putting me in charge of a bunch of humans with the same interests and maturity level as me isn't the best idea. Teachers seem so pulled together and mature. They wear sensible shoes and other adults can relate to them. There's a chance those are things they learned in college, but my gut tells me it goes beyond that. My gut also tells me I'd probably put a higher priority on snack breaks than pop quizzes, so I should probably leave the adulting to the professionals. Or, rather, the profession up to the adults. One of those, for sure.

There are many more reasons why I am happy that the twisty, bumpy path I ended up on put me exactly where I should be. I'm now a professional storyteller and a mother of kids who love books, reading, and learning just like I still do. Sometimes I get to teach grownups at writing conferences and continuing ed classes, scratching that teaching itch once in a while. Best of all, I'm jazzed to be able to support the teachers I appreciate with every fiber of my being, in the classroom and beyond, ensuring them without a doubt that I will never, *ever* try to take their jobs from them.

EVER.

KIM BONGIORNO IS THE AUTHOR AND FREELANCE WRITER BEHIND THE BLOG LET ME START BY SAYING. A CRAFTER OF EVERYTHING FROM FUNNY PARENTING TWEETS TO FANTASTICAL FICTION, HER WORK HAS RECEIVED PRAISE FROM THE LIKES OF BUZZFEED, THE TODAY SHOW, *THE HUFFINGTON POST*, AND THE ERMA BOMBECK WRITERS' WORKSHOP. KIM LIVES IN NEW JERSEY WITH HER FAMILY, WHO ARE WONDERFULLY TOLERANT OF HER BOOK HOARDING TENDENCIES. LEARN MORE AT KIMBONGIORNOWRITES.COM.

11

Home-school Dropout: A Self-Preservation Story
By Ava Mallory

"I'll homeschool him. I'm a college educated, well-read woman. I'm *totally* qualified to teach a twelve-year-old boy. I know stuff. Lots of stuff. And on the off chance I don't know something, there always the internet. Right?"

Those were the naïve ramblings of a mother with an ego bigger than her brain. That mother would be me—yours truly—the Queen of Delusions.

No one ever said I was the brightest crayon in the box. To be honest, no one ever said I was the brightest anything, but I digress...

I had a foolproof plan. The second semester would be a breeze. I, Ms. Numbskull Quack, would teach the self-righteous, habit-wearing, pseudo-educators a lesson or two. They didn't know as much as they thought they did. I could teach my son everything he needed to know. How hard could it be? (Wait for it, because the universe was about to send me an answer.)

My sweet angel would never have to step foot in the school building again if all went well inside "the dungeon" this morning. (Better not say it because some people—PTA moms, I hope your ears aren't ringing—think it's disrespectful to refer to the head honcho's office as "the dungeon." It wasn't my fault she reminded me of a fire-breathing dragon.)

I would rescue my baby from the big, bad schoolmarms with their judgmental glances and perpetually cocked eyebrows.

A quick inhale of invisible courage and I declared, "I will teach him."

The accusation against my innocent bundle of joy was an abomination. An insult to mothers everywhere. Call it mistaken identity or a misunderstanding, but no way would I let them point the finger at my boy. All I had to do was march into the principal's office and demand his release immediately. We were *so* done with this place.

There I was, Supermom, minus the cape. In hindsight, the missing cape may have been a metaphor for the other things I hadn't taken into consideration. My mother always said the absence of rational thought would lead to my demise, and as fate would have it, it did.

I grabbed the fancy, paid-for-by-my-taxpayer-dollars door handle and yanked with all my might. This was my moment to shine and then... it happened.

SNAP!

Son of a—!

Searing pain shot through my arm like a band of dagger-wielding ninjas on a Ritalin trip.

My screams were loud enough to summon a demon.

Right there. Mere seconds before my much-practiced, long-awaited Sally Field in *Norma Rae* moment of glory, my arm detached from my body.

Okay, that's a slight exaggeration, but you get the picture.

"You've got to be kidding me!"

The pain! The pain! (Channeling my inner Tattoo from Fantasy Island.)

As I was about to bellow every swear word I had in my long-curated arsenal of one-of-a-kind expletives, I spotted the camera above my head. I contemplated giving it the old one-finger salute, but my fear of being exposed as a hot-headed, irrational egomaniac and the irony of the situation (more on that later), briefly knocked sense into me.

I couldn't do it. I mean seriously. One move in the wrong direction and I'd lose my *shizz*. Labor pains (Curse you, back labor!) had nothing on this.

On the wall, inches from my nose, a sign taunted me with its large font: *Ring Bell.*

There's a safety barrier? What was wrong with me? I was a Band Booster hostage... I mean volunteer. I knew the rules. (I'm sure they mentioned them at the beginning of the year, but, I mean, seriously, does anyone really read that crap?)

After some bargaining with the big man upstairs (don't tell my mother I said that), I pushed the bell with about as much disdain as a queen who'd learned someone in her court had conspired against her.

"Open sesame, sorry suckers! You will pay for this. (I wasn't sure if I meant for disciplining my kid or for dismembering me.) Mark my words, peasants," I grumbled as I pushed the bell again to show them, I meant business.

The door buzzed. I grabbed the handle with my non-burning arm.

Would you believe the thing wouldn't budge?

Not one inch.

I tried again.

Nothing.

A gravelly woman's voice groaned from the sky, "Use both hands. The door sticks."

I stifled a whimper and moved with all the grace of Tim Conway in the dentist bit he did on the *Carol Burnett Show*. My limbs turned to jelly.

After the longest ten seconds of my life, the gravelly voice from above asked the most brilliant question of the day, "Do you need help?"

"Yes," I moaned. I leaned my back against the door and slid to the ground, cradling my right arm like it was a newborn babe. I wondered how long it would be before that child did the middle finger salute.

A few seconds later, the school secretary and the school resource officer were on the other side of the glass doors, staring at me with a mixture of pity and disgust on their faces.

I was a bawling mess on the ground, in view of a well-placed security camera.

The resource officer opened the door. "Did you fall?"

I whined like a toddler caught with her grimy fingers in the dessert, I said, "My arm hurts."

I hadn't noticed, but others were gawking at the spectacle that was me, Ms. Know It All, the mother of the accused middle-finger-wagging class clown.

"Call 9-1-1," someone said.

The resource officer was one step ahead of them, already on his radio calling for backup because nothing says, "Danger. Danger, Will Robinson" like a forty-something-year-old mother in hysterics because she got a boo-boo.

"No, don't call the police," I begged, forcing myself to my feet. "I have an appointment with Mother Teresa." (You can't make this stuff up. The school principal's chosen biblical name was Mother Teresa. Who did she think she was?)

The cop motioned for the onlookers to back away. "Don't move. An ambulance is on the way."

Obedience wasn't in my wheelhouse. I preferred to err on the side of I'm-the-mom-and-you-do-what-I-say side of life. That's where I lived.

I straightened my back and bit back the searing pain that threatened to topple me over like a herd of fainting goats. "I'm fine." He cocked an eyebrow up at me. "I have an appointment."

"To break your hip?" he asked.

I forced myself to my feet. "No. There's nothing wrong with my hips. I hurt my arm working out this morning." Why did I say that?

His gaze skimmed down my warrior princess outfit: black slacks (slimming), black tunic (always), black ballet shoes (they're the only pair that didn't give me blisters), and red lipstick (power color).

"You worked out this morning?"

It was as if I had a blind spot. I knew he was a police officer, but my ego didn't give a hoot about my freedom. It wanted vengeance.

"Listen, I birthed four babies with these hips. They're strong," I said as a dark shadow crept up and loomed over me like a bad omen. The hairs on the back of my neck stood at attention. I thought the grim reaper had come for me.

"Somehow I knew it had to be you." Mother Teresa was no Jackie Kennedy. No sweet whispers. She had the voice of a drill sergeant.

The resource officer smirked and slithered away under the guise of "waiting for the ambulance," but I bet he wanted to get a safe distance away from she-devil. Who didn't?

"Chicken," I muttered.

With a stern eye and just enough of a bottom lip to let you know she was human, Mother Teresa said, "Let's not."

I needed a doctor, but first I had to slay this dragon. "Good morning, Mother Teresa. We have a nine o'clock appointment," I said in a voice that was a cross between Lauren Bacall and Elmer Fudd because... well, pain.

Just then, the ambulance pulled into the circular drive.

"Looks like your ride is here," she said.

The driver jumped out and shouted, "What happened?"

I waved with my functioning arm. "Nothing to see here. False alarm."

The officer interjected, "I think it's her hip."

What was this guy's problem? My hips were a national treasure.

The female paramedic asked, "What happened to your hip?" She glanced around as if she'd find a wayward skateboard on the sidewalk because apparently suburban moms were into that sort of thing.

"Kill me now," I muttered. "It's not my hips. You know what? Let's pretend none of this ever happened. Sorry I wasted your time."

Yeah, no one budged.

"If you're hurt, we need to know where and how," the female paramedic said. "Did you fall?"

I didn't say it out loud, but I thought it. *No. I didn't fall, Knockoff Barbie. I came down with a sudden case of middle-age-ness and my freakin' arm fell out of the socket. Now, can you back off, so I can read the Dragon Lady and her team of half-baked know-it-alls the riot act for placing my kid in in-school suspension?*

"No one fell!" I screeched through gritted teeth.

"Then how did you hurt your hip?" the male paramedic asked.

I wanted to rip their eyeballs out of their big, dumb heads, but since I only had one arm left, I didn't want to risk it. "Jesus Christ Superstar! I. DID. NOT. HURT. MY. HIP!" I took the deepest deep breath I could muster under the circumstances and forced a different tone to come out of my mouth. "I hurt my arm. It's fine. Don't worry about me. Everything is under control. (Famous last words of a drama queen.) The Mother and I have a meeting."

She narrowed her beady blue eyes at me. "The Mother?"

I gulped. Catholic guilt was no joke. "Sorry. Mother Teresa, the fake one, not the other one. The other one is dead." I made the sign of the cross as if it'd save me.

What was wrong with me? Why couldn't I shut my pie hole?

The officer and the bewildered paramedics commiserated while the dear Mother and her entire administrative team escorted me into the building.

"Can she go, Thomas?" Mother Teresa stopped at the door.

Officer Not-So-Friendly shrugged. "I guess."

"Wait," the paramedic said. "We need you to sign something."

What?

After I signed my life away, I followed the Queen Bee into her office that overlooked the front drive, photos of three Pope's plastered on the walls and waited for her to make the first move.

She didn't hesitate. "I know why you're here. Your offspring (she didn't say offspring, but it was implied) told me you plan to home-school him."

I opened my mouth to explain, but she hushed me with a wave of her hand.

"While I can't say I'm thrilled to hear that news, I can't say I'm surprised."

"What?" What was that supposed to mean?

She shrugged. "You're not the first mother who came in here to tell me how we've wronged their child." She slid into her seat. "It's the trend now. Parents think they can handle it."

"I can. It's not like it's hard."

She smirked. "It's not as easy as you might think."

I glanced at the ceiling, sure this B was messing with me.

She leaned forward, her long, thin arms folded in front of her slender frame. "It truly isn't. I can't tell you how many mothers and fathers who've pulled their child out of school, then returned a short time later, begging us to re-enroll them."

Someone alert Charlie Sheen because she thinks she's totally winning this *mofo*.

"Well, that won't happen with us. I'm fully prepared to home-school him." I wasn't, but she didn't need to know that.

"You want what's best for your son, don't you?"

What I wanted was a shot glass full of Valium and a long nap.

"Yes," I managed.

Finally, she motioned for me to sit. "Given his excitability and his—"

I had to stop her there. I'd heard this sad song before, and I didn't like it.

"Hold up. With all due respect, Sister, I think I know what's best for my child." I summoned the strength of my ancestors. "My precious baby (I called him by his name, obviously, but you get the picture) may not be perfect, but I hardly think a mere accusation should warrant a suspension. I will educate him." Her eyebrows lifted so high, I couldn't discern the differ-ence between her habit (the one on her head, not the lip curling thing) and her actual, albeit receding hairline. "I'm qualified."

The smirk returned to her face. "Ms.—"

The office door opened behind me.

Great. Reinforcements. That's all I needed.

"Hello," the woman–let's call her Middle School Math Teacher Ratched, as in Nurse Ratched, except instead of a sharp needle, she had an angry red pen that she used liberally-poked her head in the door. "I'm so glad I caught you."

I turned too quickly and slammed my right arm against Mother May I's desk. "Fudge stick on a... Son of a..." I wracked my brain to come up with an appropriate turn of phrase that wouldn't offend my holier-than-thou hosts. I'd already come to terms with spending eternity begging for forgiveness for my potty mouth, but the last thing I needed was a one-way ticket to Hades. Not alone anyway.

"Are you okay? Did you hurt yourself?" she asked.

I wish I could say I sucked up the excruciating pain and gave them the what for, but that would be a big, fat lie. I cried like a baby. "It hurts so bad."

The nurse knelt next to me and lifted my sleeve, exposing a giant bruise on the inside of my arm. "Oh my. You really hurt yourself. Haven't you?" The little girl in me sobbed harder. "Does it hurt when I do this?" She moved it a little. I winced in pain. "My husband is Dr. Ratched (not his name), the orthopedic surgeon. I'm no expert, but I think you may have torn or sprained something. Would you like me to call an ambulance for you?"

Mother Teresa made a noise. I remember it as being a snort, but let's pretend she had a heart and groaned in sympathy for me. "The ambulance was here. She refused treatment."

Ratched didn't flinch. "Okay. Would you like us to call them back?"

"Yes," my voice shook like I was on a Tilt-a-Whirl. "Please."

Within seconds, The Habit and Ratched had assembled a team of faux Florence Nightingales. One poured a fresh cup of coffee for me. Another phoned an emergency contact listed on my son's school file.

Another summoned Officer Not-So-Friendly, who sauntered in with a Cheshire cat grin on his face like this was part of his master plan.

"You're all so sweet. I can't believe it," I said.

"You can't? Why not?" Ratched asked.

A rational person would think before she answered. I think we'd already established I was anything but rational.

"Because you are evil people who punish kids for being kids."

The collective gasp sucked the oxygen out of the room.

"Evil? Punish kids?" Mother Teresa stood, towering above me like a wolf ready to attack its prey.

I swallowed my pain and stood to face her and diffuse the situation. "I didn't mean that. It's the pain talking. Not me. I should go to confession." I rambled like a buffoon. "Did you know I haven't been to confession since my sister's wedding? I should probably do something about that."

The nurse saved me again. "Your arm." She pointed to my limp arm. "Doesn't it hurt when you do that?"

I glanced down at it, then up at Mother Heifer, and quickly calculated how badly I'd screwed up this whole situation. "It hurts so bad."

Ratched pulled a cell phone out of her pant's pocket. "Calling 9-1-1."

Mother Teresa glanced out the window. "Put the phone down. You don't have to do that." She opened a window and shouted. "We need help up here. Her arm hurts. Again."

The paramedics looked just as happy to see me again as I thought they would when they carried their gear into the office.

"Hey, guys!" I said as I scrubbed the tears from my face. "Turns out I need your help."

"No kidding," the female paramedic said.

"Dying here," I said. "Funny story. I came here to tell these old bats I didn't appreciate how they treated my kid and they ended up helping me. Isn't that funny?"

Mother Teresa opened her mouth to say something, but Ratched gave her a beautifully crafted side eye and made her swallow her words.

While the paramedics assessed my injury, I reconsidered. I had every intention of making them pay for defaming my baby boy. I wanted heads to roll. My child flipped off a surveillance camera. (At least I checked for a camera first.) But a near fatal accident (I told you I was dramatic) made me rethink.

Maybe the old biddies weren't so bad.

"Here's what will happen," the female paramedic started. "You need to see a doctor and get an X-ray. Can we offer you a lift?" She nodded to her partner. "How does that sound?"

Mother Teresa clapped her hands in a slow-motion golf clap. "So, are we done here?"

I won't lie. I wanted to say something witty, but the pain numbed my tongue.

Teacher Ratched placed a gentle hand on my shoulder. "I really enjoy having your spawn (she used his given name) in class. He's a smart kid."

"He is?" Tears sprang from my eyes again.

She nodded. "Oh, the middle finger thing? That's nothing compared to some things I've seen. In fact, I've flipped off inanimate objects from time to time too." She threw in a wink just to add salt to my already wounded ego.

How wrong was I about her?

Way wrong.

The paramedics escorted me out of the office.

"Wait." I glanced over my shoulder. "That whole pulling my kid out-of-school thing. Can we pretend like it never happened?"

"You want to keep your son enrolled?" I wished Mother Teresa didn't look so pleased with herself.

"Yes," I said.

She offered a full smile, teeth and all.

Say nothing. Say nothing.

She and Ratched exchanged glances.

"Yes, I want him to remain enrolled here... at this school... with you." Swallowing my pride hurt worse than my arm. I wondered if the doctors had a cure for swallowing crow. Probably not.

. . .

AVA MALLORY IS A MULTI-GENRE *USA TODAY* AND *WALL STREET JOURNAL* BESTSELLING AUTHOR. WHEN NOT DREAMING UP STORIES, SHE CAN BE FOUND CHAUFFEURING HER MIDDLE SCHOOLER OR WALKING THE TIGHTROPE BETWEEN SMOTHERING HER YOUNG ADULT AND ADULT CHILDREN OR LETTING THEM ROAM FREE WHILE SHE DOCUMENTS IT ON HER BLOG.

12

Ill Composition
By Victoria Fedden

There is no experience on earth that will make you feel uncool and irrelevant faster than standing in front of a room of nearly thirty college freshman and trying to teach them how to write. Albeit, only about fifteen of them will actually notice you, because the rest of them will be glued to their smartphones, but still. And yet I subject myself to this torture five days a week for several hours straight. Am I crazy? Probably. But I really love my job, and not just for all the vacation time. Teaching is fun, creative, dynamic, and totally rewarding, so I can't imagine doing anything else, even if the job is a bit crushing to my self-esteem at times.

We educators are the victims of some pretty inaccurate stereotypes. As a female English professor, I have it particularly bad. During a recent lesson on stereotypes, I asked my class what assumptions they could make about me based on appearance alone. Big mistake. They said I only watch Lifetime movies, listen to audio-books, and have a lot of cats. Everyone thinks I'm Lilith from *Cheers* over here, and if I were in a movie, I'd surely be portrayed as frigid, alone, and suited in head-to-toe tweed. For the record, I do not own a single item of tweed clothing and that's definitely intentional. Also for the record, it might be true that I can get unnecessarily fired up about Modernist poets, so maybe some stereotypes are a little bit true, but I swear I'm not actually a cold-hearted introvert. I'm a complex human being.

Of course, my students would be shocked to learn that I'm a real person, because they think I'm a magical writing machine that resides permanently in the classroom. A few semesters ago, after learning that several in my class worked at Chipotle, I decided to pay them a visit, and you should have seen the looks on their faces. I think they were deeply shaken that I exist off-campus, and that I actually eat. As I wolfed down my burrito bowl, I could see them huddled together whispering and pointing, like "OMG, she even knows that guac costs extra! How is that possible?"

My students think I've never heard of anything. Their favorite game is wasting time during lectures and group work by asking me if I know about stuff they think is cool and subversive.

"I'm trying to teach you how to formulate a decent thesis," I say with a dramatic eye roll.

"We know, miss, but come on, have you ever heard of Kendrick Lamar?" they demand.

So I tell them to sit down and be humble and they all simultaneously die while I gloat.

In addition to never having heard of anything, my students also think I've never *done* anything. These kids have no clue that I like music and swear and have occasionally engaged in acts of debauchery, since they believe me to be a virginal, religious prude who attends church services while wearing heavy layers of modest clothing. Like all teachers do, of course.

I will never forget years ago when I had to tell them that I was pregnant to explain my constant puking and why I couldn't teach a class without sipping a smoothie. After I made the big announcement there were none of the expected cheers of congratulations and excitement for new life. Nope. Instead, I could literally see every single one of them thinking in horror "SHE HAD SEX," and then wondering if there was any other possible way I could have gotten pregnant because there was no way Miss Fedden could have ever done something like have sex because no one over twenty-five does that and teachers never do it because teachers are pillars of chastity.

I really shouldn't indulge their nonsense, but deep down I secretly want to be the "cool teacher," which is exactly like "the cool mom," except worse.

When I teach I like to incorporate a lot of different pop culture references—things I hope my students can relate to, so they stay interested and engaged, but also so I can look less like someone who watches Lifetime movies with her thirty-five cats. I do okay with this most of the time, but every once in a while I'll bring something up that I had thought was cool and hip only to learn that nope, it wasn't at all and I was just another adult pretending I was down with the eighteen-year-olds. My heart broke when someone wrote on Rate My Professor that I tried to act young, because, wait, I thought I was, wasn't I and wasn't I just acting like myself? I finally had to face the sad fact that while I saw myself as young and cool and entirely with it despite being in my forties, that my students saw me as outdated, nerdy, and kind of pathetic. I may as well have been saying, "Gnarly, dude."

One day, though, I finally got my chance to be cool.

I don't remember exactly how the Beastie Boys came up in my Intro to Comp class, but we were discussing rap lyrics, and I mentioned one of their songs.

Twenty-six blank faces stared at me in confused silence until one kid came out with it.

"Miss," he said, "WHO are the Beastie *whatevers*?"

This kid was eighteen, had just moved here from Queens, and was obsessed with rap and hip-hop. I figured he, of all the students, would surely know who the Beastie Boys were. But nope.

"'Brass Monkey'? 'Sure Shot'?" I suggested weakly.

More blank stares.

"Yeah, miss, are they like a Christian group or something?" another girl asked.

Stunned. I was stunned. I had to sit down to process that my students, who, I just realized had never lived in a world without high-speed Internet, did not know who the Beastie Boys were. And while I was at it, a girl just asked me if they were a Christian group. Seriously? What the F kind of a Christian group would call themselves anything with the word "beast" in it for God's sakes? Of all the stupid questions my students had asked me, that was definitely in the top five, but I didn't tell her that.

"Umm, technically I think they're Jewish, actually," I said, "They're rappers."

Hilarity. The whole class laughed. Jewish rappers, hahahahaha.

"No, really," said another kid, "Jewish rappers? That's a thing?"

"They are actually among the greatest rappers who have ever lived," I said. "They were visionaries."

The class looked at me like I was straight up smoking crack at my podium.

"You listen to Jewish rappers, miss?" The kid from New York asked with a look of absolute disgust.

Someone made a joke about their songs being about bar mitzvahs, and that was when I'd had it.

When you go to school to become a teacher, they're always talking about the importance of finding teachable moments, seizing those moments, and turning them into valuable learning experiences that resonate with students' lives. Well, this was one of those opportunities. Forget my lesson about the importance of transition words, and to hell with trying to teach them to stop writing run-on sentences. We had more important work to do that day.

I dropped everything, fired up the projector, pulled down the movie screen, and spent the rest of the period showing Beastie Boys videos and discussing them. Homework: listen to *all* of *Paul's Boutique* and write a response to it.

Many people would say, *really*? Shouldn't you have taught your students about pronoun antecedent disagreement? Wouldn't your time have been better spent drilling into their heads for the seventy-ninth time that the period goes outside of the parentheses?

To this I say no. I am a teacher and I owed those kids a good education. On that day they got it, and I finally got my wish to be cool. The next time that class met, they actually thanked me for introducing them to some truly genius music, even if it was "old school."

"You must've been like us back in your day," one girl said.

I shrugged.

"Maybe," I said, "I guess I'm just old now."

"You're not old, miss. You're the OG!" Mr. New York said.

I may have blushed a little. It was one of the best compliments I've ever gotten from a student, but I played it off.

"Okay, okay, can we get back to writing conclusions now?" I laughed.

VICTORIA FEDDEN IS A WRITER AND A MOM FROM FORT LAUDERDALE, FLORIDA. HER MEMOIR *THIS IS NOT MY BEAUTIFUL LIFE* WAS PUBLISHED JUNE 2016 BY PICADOR USA. SHE RECEIVED HER MFA IN CREATIVE WRITING FROM FLORIDA ATLANTIC UNIVERSITY IN 2009, AND NOW TEACHES COLLEGE WRITING. HER ESSAYS AND ARTICLES HAVE APPEARED IN *REAL SIMPLE, CHICKEN SOUP FOR THE SOUL, THE HUFFINGTON POST, REDBOOK, ELEPHANT JOURNAL*, SCARY MOMMY, BABBLE AND *THE SOUTH FLORIDA SUN SENTINEL*, PLUS VARIOUS OTHER PUBLICATIONS.

13

Teachers as Parents
By Mai Wen

I bet you think you know what this essay will be about by the title. You'll think both my parents were teachers and I'm going to tell you about how many late nights they stayed up grading papers or worrying about their students or stressing about angry parents.

The truth is my mom was a nurse and then computer programmer, and my dad was more often than not unemployed. And they both were horrible at teaching anything. My mom's teaching style included telling me something in as few words as possible, with absolutely no explanation, and getting really pissed when I didn't understand it like *right* away. And then she was done with me. I was deemed unteachable and too ignorant for her attention.

My father was similar. He only gave me one shot at learning something before his calm would turn as sharp and cold as winter in Minnesota and he'd use pain to teach me. I wasn't catching the football? Well then, he'd throw the ball as hard as he could at my face, often causing a bloody nose. But no tears, because tears brought on even more of his wrath. I couldn't pick up the rhythm of a song? Then, naturally, he'd pick me up by my neck and bang my head on the wall to the beat of the song. My father was passionate about his sports, music and anger.

I didn't have a good Kindergarten teacher, so we will skip over her (let's just say it involved me having to sit in the corner many times as punishment for mixing Mandarin with my English, and her telling my mother to stop speaking to me in Mandarin). But it was my first-grade teacher that I still remember and who made me realize what teachers could be for me.

His name was Mr. Nelson and I was terrified of him. From my experience, adults were scary and the male adults hurt you. I don't know if this is insulting at all to Mr. Nelson, but for some reason I remember him resembling Gilbert Gottfried. He was a little man with dark brown curls at an appropriately 1980s hair length. I remember he wore sweaters and khaki pants every day, even in the spring when the weather started to slowly warm up (it was Minnesota, after all). For much of my first grade I avoided him and kept my head down. Then one day he motioned for me to join him at his desk. Terrified —*what had I done wrong?*—I made my way to him with slow, hesitant steps. He crouched down to my level and leaned close. My heart felt like it was on the verge of stopping cold.

"I heard about your parents getting divorced. Please let me know if you need someone to talk to or if you just need a hug. Okay?" His voice, which was usually bubbly and upbeat, was quiet and gentle. His brown eyes kind. Still, I was scared. Would he make me hug him? He did not. He stood up after I nodded my understanding and left me alone.

My mother wasn't much of a hugger. If you tried to hug her, she'd either stiffen and let her arms hang limp or awkwardly pat your back in a *yeah, yeah, let's just get this over with* sort of way. With my father, physical contact was confusing and often involved pain. But for some reason, after he suggested it, I wanted a hug from Mr. Nelson. It seemed like it might be different. Eventually, one day, I worked up the courage to ask for a hug. He was kind and warm, without hurting me or making me feel uncomfortable. It wasn't hurried and too short, nor was it long and uncomfortably lingering. It was just right and a knowledge grew in me. Two things, really. One was that not all adults were scary, and two was that I not only wanted positive physical contact with adults, a part of me needed it, and it wasn't something I'd ever get at home.

After Mr. Nelson I was quick to trust, and hug, my teachers.

In fourth grade I had seen a coveted marker a classmate had received for his birthday. It was cerulean blue, the most beautiful blue I'd ever seen, and had three tips so when you drew with it three beautiful parallel lines marked the paper like a flowing river. So I stole it. Unfortunately another student saw me take it and told on me. My teacher, Ms. Clark, actually kind of scared me. She was one that I hadn't quite sucked up to as much as some previous teachers. Partially because she wasn't the hugging type and I lived to hug my teachers, but also because she was strict. When she pulled me aside to talk to me about the stolen marker, I was sure she was going to hate me and be so disappointed. Instead she told me that she knew I was a good kid and that everybody made bad choices from time to time, what was important was to learn from them.

I remember staring at her in shock. So she didn't hate me and think I was the most horrible human being in the world? At home, every mistake was met with harsh punishment and a heavy mantle of disappointment. This was new. I'd never gotten in trouble at school before (except for in Kindergarten for kissing boys on the bus, but that's another story) and didn't often after this incident. But I always remembered how Ms. Clark didn't condemn me, but encouraged the good inside of me. It was one thing for teachers to see me as good when I was sucking up to them and not getting into trouble, but Ms. Clark still saw me as good even after I did something bad. I warmed up to her considerably after that incident, even squeezing a hug out of her on the last day of school, much to her surprise.

There are other teachers I remember or wish I remembered better. My third-grade teacher, Ms. Gilmore, who was my teacher pen pal. I found out when I was in fifth grade that she was diagnosed with cancer so I sent every cent I owned (literally, you have no idea how many stamps I had to use on that envelope) to her in the mail to help pay for her treatment. Her letter of thanks is one I wish I still had. I remember feeling as if I'd never been thanked properly before that letter. Her gratefulness was so profuse and genuine, overflowing off the page and into my heart. She did get better, I remember.

I had a male math teacher in middle school who I only remember as Mr. Gacky (that doesn't sound like a real name to me, so I have to think it was a nickname). I remember watching him joke with one of my classmates. The classmate would make fun of his sweaters, saying "Is the circus in town and did you steal a sweater from them?" and he would joke back, saying something like, "I didn't steal from the circus because I'm *in* the circus, didn't you see me after your act?" The shock that coursed through me that an adult would allow a child to talk to him that way took me the entire school year to process. A yearning grew in me to joke with Mr. Gacky as well. I'd think of variations of the jokes my classmate and Mr. Gacky made to each other, but in the end I never said any of these out loud. Afraid I'd get it wrong and actually make him mad; the secret to joking with adults was beyond my courage and understanding. But still, it gave me a strange happiness to see my classmate and teacher joke with each other, even if I was an outsider just looking in. And once again my ideas on adult-child interactions shifted.

I had another male teacher in middle school who was kind, Mr. Nguyen, making me fear men a little bit less. And a female teacher whose name I'm so sad I don't remember, but I can see her in my mind, who recommended me for a Young Writer's Conference. Her choosing me and going to the conference gave me the confidence to take my dream of becoming a writer seriously.

In high school I certainly had stopped hugging my teachers, but they didn't stop stepping in when I needed them most. At this point my dad wasn't in my life physically, but the damage he'd done was wreaking havoc. I was depressed, suicidal, partaking in risky behaviors, and I felt so alone, damaged, and dirty. I can't remember exactly how my Creative Writing teacher found out about my father's abuse of me, I may have written about it in a journal or short story for Ms. Nichols' class, but I remember her sitting with me in the hallway and not making me feel dirty or ashamed at all. In fact, she made me feel brave and strong. Like I could tackle my trauma, I could get through it. When I submitted a poem about my abuse to the school literary magazine, she made sure I was okay with the fact that the deeper meaning of the poem may be understood by some. I was. I had found my courage and strength, partly in thanks to her. She has continued to support my writing and healing to this day.

My struggles continued in college and I had a teacher, Shi Laoshi, who let me make up a final because I was wandering the winter streets in distress after my father unexpectedly contacted me. Many of my teachers not only excused my absences because I literally couldn't get out of bed due to my depression, but would call to check on me, making sure I was okay.

I had a creative writing teacher, Mr. Bauer, who to this day I not only trust to guide me in my writing, but also in life. I was still afraid of male teachers, though I tried very hard not to be, and I feel Mr. Bauer understood this about me early on. Mr. Bauer knew about my childhood trauma because I wrote about it and he handled it exactly right. He was careful and kind with me, while still being a good, honest creative writing instructor. He took the time to get to know me, lent me books (I still cringe remembering how I accidentally tore the book jacket on one), met with me to talk about writing and checked in on me when he could tell I was struggling. You could feel how he cared about his students, not just their writing--which he was very passionate about—but also as people he wanted to get to know. Students loved him so much we'd all sign up for each consecutive class of his, forming a little group that we called the "Bauerians." I am still friends with many of the other Bauerians. His class encouraged a closeness amongst the students that formed lasting friendships (and in two of my friends' cases, a wedding!) Not only did he help me grow exponentially as a writer, but he was the first teacher I honestly felt I could call a friend.

Yes, my teachers taught me stuff like calculus, grammar, and chemistry, a lot of which I've honestly forgotten (sorry, teachers!) But that's not what I remember about my teachers. I remember the teachers being there in ways that I hadn't realized I needed; less as teachers and more like parents. They filled in holes that were left empty in me from my own parents. It's something that isn't asked of or expected of teachers, but just looking at my history, you can see how many teachers do so without hesitation.

I've often wondered how I would have turned out without my teachers. When I look back on my childhood I remember my teachers as the stable force in my life. The people I could go to when I needed to feel seen, safe and valued. With my home life I could have taken many darker paths than what I did. I heavily flirted with some of those paths at times, but school was always my lighthouse. Guiding me to possibilities and a future I often had a hard time conjuring up on my own. Without teachers I have no doubt I would have been lost, diving deep into the darkness of my trauma and disappearing for good. But teachers held my hand, hugged me, loved me, taught me, and whether they ever knew it, saved me.

MAI WEN IS A FORMER SOCIAL WORKER AND CURRENT WRITER. SHE IS A CONTRIBUTOR TO *YOU DO YOU* FROM THE POPULAR *I JUST WANT TO PEE ALONE* SERIES. SHE IS ALSO AN ASPIRING NOVELIST WITH TWO COMPLETED YOUNG ADULT SCIENCE FICTION MANUSCRIPTS AND WORKING ON AN ADULT FANTASY. HER NOVELS CONTAIN STRONG SOCIAL, WOMEN'S AND MENTAL HEALTH ISSUES BUT WITH A DOSE OF TIME TRAVEL OR SCIENCEY MAGIC (PICK YOUR POISON, SHE'S GOT BOTH). IF INTERESTED IN LEARNING MORE ABOUT HER WORK, YOU CAN FIND HER ON SOCIAL MEDIA @MAIWENWRITER.

14

Impact
By Stefani Kerwin

I t has been a long day. One week ago, while eating dinner after a long day of volleyball and basketball, I received an email from the principal of our middle school. I shared the news with my family that Mrs. Smith, Emma's seventh-grade math teacher, who was also her eighth-grade volleyball coach, had suddenly passed away that morning. To say we were stunned would be a ridiculous understatement.

Today we attended her funeral. Not my daughter's first, but now that she is older, it was definitely more impactful.

Mrs. Smith was only twenty-nine, and a beautiful soul. I am grieving for her husband, her little boy left behind, the little one who went with her, and also for my daughter. It was so hard to watch her fight through tears to sing, honoring her teacher, as our middle school choir performed. I am so proud of her.

I took away a few things.

Nothing is promised. We call it the present, because that's what it is ... a gift. Every day is a gift. Share your love every day. Mrs. Smith had only been married for two years, and her son isn't even a year-old yet. Even in that short time, she made sure her family knew just how much she loved them, each and every day.

Have a servant's heart. Do things for others, just because. It doesn't have to be a grand gesture ... small things can have just as much impact. Mrs. Smith made herself available every day before and after school to meet with students who were struggling with math. Her husband talked about how she would spend time every evening brainstorming on how best to serve her students. She even tutored students from other schools. Her thoughts were always of others before herself. My daughter is excelling in math this year, and I know it is due to the good foundation Mrs. Smith gave her last year.

Be kind. It costs nothing but can be everything. You never know what someone else might be going through and just how much a kind word can make their day, or even turn their life around. This world would be so much better if we were all kind.

Mrs. Smith's classroom will soon be occupied by another teacher. She cannot be replaced, though someone else will be taking over her duties at school. The edges of the ragged hole left behind will be softened over time. The memories of her positive attitude, her beautiful smile and overwhelming drive to give her best to her students every day will live on.

My thoughts and prayers are with Mrs. Smith's family, our school community, and everyone else who had the good fortune to know her. We volunteered at Harvesters and lit a candle at Mass today, and spent some time celebrating her life.

Emma told me that she and her friends have been saying, "What would Mrs. Smith do?" when they have a dilemma. As a coach, she was very positive and supportive of her players. My daughter has dedicated the remainder of her club volleyball season to her. As a teacher, she was deeply committed to her students. As a person, she was kind and supportive and loving. I can't think of a better guide.

. . .

STEFANI KERWIN IS A FIRST-TIME WRITER, AND COMPUTER PROGRAMMER BY TRADE. SHE IS A MARRIED MOM OF TWO MIDDLE SCHOOLERS WHO PLAY COMPETITIVE SPORTS, SO DRIVING AND SITTING ARE A BIG PART OF HER LIFE.

15

Fifth Grade
By Katelyn Sullivan

I f you can put up with twenty-plus children, seven hours a day, five times a week, two hundred days a year, then I respect you. Teachers don't get enough admiration. They struggle through long weeks, waiting for the weekend; even then, they sometimes dedicate their free hours to us. They teach and reteach concepts that may be insanely easy to them, but incomprehensible to us, the students.

I've heard horror stories about some teachers, how your year would be a living nightmare to be taught by them. And, although I hate to admit it, I've been gullible enough to believe other students in that a teacher is a demon. But, believe me: it's almost never the teacher. It's usually the student- or, worse, the parent.

I'm a relatively quiet person, and only talk if I'm with a close friend or if something catches my attention. So I've experienced first-hand the horrible things students have done to teachers. Talking back happens on a regular basis, not listening to instructions is a common occurrence, and most frequently my peers fool around with friends.

Although I prefer to see myself as a model student, I am not guiltless. No student is perfect, nor am I myself. Doubtlessly I've talked to friends during class or argued with a peer. We all have our faults.

Symmetrically, teachers aren't flawless. But there are some who are pretty close.

I'D HEARD about Mrs. Malec. Both my sisters had her, whether for math or homeroom. I met her once or twice, but what I never expected is how she would change my life. She has a presence that makes you know that she's in charge and not to mess with her, but she isn't frightening. She's creative and silly, but not even close to childish. And she's truthful.

I've discovered with adults that truthfulness is a trait that is found rarely. It's not their fault; sometimes it *is* important to stretch and bend the truth. Once in a while, though, it's nice to escape the fantasy world built up around us by adults and get a piece of truth; not stark reality, but sincerity.

Although I did just say that Mrs. Malec was impeccable, I'm sure she did have flaws, even if I never saw them. She put up with everyone, all while maintaining a friendly disposition. She gave us freedom, and opportunities to voice our own opinions. She quite literally made the environment warm by knitting and crocheting blankets while she talked, many in patterns and colors of our suggestions.

I have never met another person like her. Mrs. Malec managed to teach us without making us feel ludicrous or dumb. Many times a staff member would walk in to our room and stare at the things we did—singing loudly and off-tune about math and Latin, dancing around the room, or burying ourselves under layers of blankets. Often, one could catch the twenty-some of us in the open air library, talking animatedly and unashamedly hugging dozens of stuffed animals.

She taught my friends and I to have no shame—we quickly became fearless of how we looked to others, laughing out loud easily and carrying on despite the looks we were given. Mrs. Malec taught us to appreciate what we have—our youth and friends, the futures laid out before us.

Through this, without knowing it, she helped me through the struggle with another person in the grade. Unfortunately, my time in elementary was spent battling an enemy, a bully. Mrs. Malec taught me to stand up for myself and be unafraid of what others thought of me, which led me to stand up to this other person.

The one time we did disappoint her—which every child knows is much worse than angering an adult- shame filled every single one of my classmates to the core. I don't think we talked that day, just stumbled around, pale, in a useless stupor. Mrs. Malec's respect meant everything to us, and without it, we were lost. In fact, the rest of the week we were especially careful of what we said or did. With that experience, we learned respect is one of the most important gifts someone can give you.

Despite all she's taught me, Mrs. Malec's greatest achievement was being able to teach me math. It may seem insignificant compared to everything else this wonderful woman has done for me, but I *loathe* the subject. My hatred for math makes it harder for me to learn it, my brain blocking the numbers and figures out of my head. And yet, somehow, I was in advanced math.

To help my classmates and I remember different solutions, she came up with jingles. Even now, almost three years later, they still dance through my head, easily replaying themselves. During tests, problems test me with complicated and recollection, and the little songs help me, their catchy tunes making me smile.

Everything she's given me and taught me is nothing compared to the memories I received along the way. Two in particular stand out, since they were events the grade prepared for all year.

The Dig. The class was split in two, and then told to create a country, a town, a continent--some type of society. Being uncreative eleven-year-olds, my group, which I was in charge of, was christened South Antarctica.

Over the next few weeks each class in the grade made their own societies, each with their own religions, regions, currencies, governments, and so on. It was rigorous work that brought our groups together. It was incredibly difficult, and we only had a short amount of time to create the entire thing.

It was the beginning of the year, so I was still unused to and wary of my new classmates.

For some, it may have been unbearable; in fact, many other classes in the grade hated the entire thing, having to spend hours on end with people they barely knew or hadn't seen in a long time. But the creators of South Antarctica had Mrs. Malec, who made the experience five times better by giving us pointers and making us laugh, as well as having us use teamwork to solve issues that would come up while in the process of making our government.

If not for another event later that year, it would have been the highlight of fifth grade, which is saying a lot, since fifth was the best year of school I've ever had. That is *including* kindergarten, which had nap time, unanimously the best class you can take. By the end of creating South Antarctica, I had a great appreciation for what it takes to make and run a government and country—and had made new friends along the way.

The project had a point, which many weren't too sure to be excited about or not. Personally, I thought the idea was smart—each group creates ten artifacts which then are hidden in baby pools filled with mulch and dirt. The goal was for another country to uncover the artifacts like archaeologists and then try and decipher exactly when the items had been created, the language of the country, and other details.

This section of the project was much harder than it seemed— harder then the creation of the societies. It was difficult for some kids, including myself, to have the creations they had worked on for weeks on end destroyed in the mud and mulch. But when the day for discovering came around, everyone's artifacts were eventually buried.

The week after the Dig was spent brainstorming what each artifact we had uncovered was for and decoding plaques and paragraphs. We worked for long periods of time, Mrs. Malec helping us piece together information and solving minor disagreements.

I'm doubtful the experience would've been half as fun without her.

The Dig was a minor event compared to Medieval Day, an entire day dedicated to the Middle Ages. It was hyped up for years before we actually participated it in. I don't know a single person who didn't look forward to it for at least half of their elementary school career.

Once again, classes were split in two. Each half of a class created a kingdom that had a king a queen, a knight, a squire, and other roles in a royal court. In that, I became a coin maker, designing three types of coins that would be used later in a medieval fair.

The next three weeks were a whirlwind of five foot tall banners, narwhals, speeches, and debates over kingdom names. Being the "creative" kids we were, we took a classic kingdom—Camelot—and flipped the name. In the end, Tolemac emerged, a united kingdom complete with royals, government, and currencies.

On a sweltering May day, Medieval Day was held. There were parades around the school, kingdoms proudly showing off lords and ladies in thick woolen clothing and jesters and knights in flashy finery. Of course they were all made small in comparison to "the Goddess"—an ostentatious Mrs. Malec in a shimmering turquoise blue dress. A feast was held in the cafeteria, which the planners had attempted to dub a "hall," featuring meats, cakes, and vegetables.

If you ignored the ninety degree weather, it was one of the best days of my life. There was a fair held later in the day, where kids would partner up and "sell" products to their classmates. Luckily for the grade, my best friend Rory and I had been brainstorming for months on what to sell with our fake kingdom currency, and finally settled on floats. As you'd imagine, we were quickly overrun, our root beer, cream soda, and "purple cow" floats disappearing like magic.

And yet, the most enjoyable part of it wasn't the candy and ice cream, nor the memories made along the way. It was the sight of our teacher flouncing around the fair, a large ball gown swishing at her feet, armed with a colorful variety of fake jewel currency.

Words can describe virtually anything in the world—emotions, places, thoughts. And yet, with hundreds, thousands, *millions* of words in existence, I don't believe there is a single word or sentence I can use to express my appreciation and admiration for Mrs. Ann Malec.

KATELYN SULLIVAN IS A THIRTEEN-YEAR-OLD LIVING OUTSIDE THE WASHINGTON, DC, AREA. THIS IS HER SECOND PUBLICATION, HAVING PREVIOUSLY BEEN PUBLISHED IN *YOU DO YOU*. SHE IS A GIRL SCOUT, A HORSEBACK RIDER, AND PLAYS VOLLEYBALL, BASKETBALL, AND LACROSSE. SHE LIVES WITH HER TWO SISTERS, PARENTS, DOG, AND CAT.

16

Beyond the Test
By Kelly Greenway

Recently my seven-year-old son asked me what high school was like. Talk about a loaded question.

For a moment, I flashed back to the field parties with bonfires and Bud Lights (yeah, I grew up in the South), the devastation of unrequited love (fucker), and the seemingly never-ending pile of homework that prevented me from watching MTV every second of my waking hours. But I didn't think that's the kind of answer that would really serve a second grader. "High school," I explained in my most measured mom voice, "is a different experience for everyone. It depends on what school you go to, how comfortable you feel there, who your friends are (or aren't), and lots of other things you can't really understand until you experience it." #nailedit

"Did you like your teacher?" he asked. "Well," I said, "in high school, you don't just have one teacher a year like you do now. You have lots. And some of them you'll love and probably some of them you won't, but they all have lessons to teach you. They can all make a difference in your life. Oh, and high school will also be better if you don't do drugs."

Okay, I didn't say that last part, but I sure as hell thought it. I'm not saying I never tried drugs, I'm just saying there was a rumor about a guy in my high school who did so many drugs that he couldn't leave his house because he thought he was a glass of orange juice and if he moved he would spill all over the floor. So, yeah, best just to stay away if you ask me.

This conversation prompted me to think back on some of my high school teachers. If you've never done this exercise, I highly recommend taking a few minutes to do so. It's a fascinating walk down memory lane, and I can almost guarantee that you'll feel differently about a few of them now that you've gotten some distance and perspective under your belt. Some teachers can only truly be appreciated through hindsight.

My Latin teacher, for instance, who lived and breathed everything there is to live and breathe about a language that, most would argue, is dead. Her joy over teaching us the differences between Doric, Ionic, and Corinthian columns was truly unparalleled. Unfortunately for me, they all looked exactly the same, except maybe one of them had a curly doohickey at the top? I really can't be sure. I took three years of Latin from her, and though I probably should have chosen, I don't know, ANY language other than that to learn, I still think back with such appreciation about the time she told me, after a class exercise where we came up with questions to ask other students, that I could be the next Barbara Walters. Not coincidentally, interviewing people in any capacity is one of my absolute favorite things to do. Though I am still waiting for my shot on *The View*.

Or my quirky, mad scientist-looking ninth-grade science teacher who made my least favorite subject something I actually loved through his unique lens and wicked sense of humor. There was also my twelfth-grade English teacher who helped me master the five-paragraph essay and allowed me to write a paper on whether or not Hamlet had an Oedipus Complex (spoiler alert: he did). There are so many teachers, and so many memories, that make me grateful for my high school experience, even now, twenty years later.

But it's one teacher I had in the eleventh grade who I don't believe I could forget even if I tried. I was having trouble concentrating in her AP (Advanced Placement) history class, which wasn't normally my style. Though we were nearing the end of the semester, and the AP exam that we'd been preparing for all year to earn college credit was only a few weeks away, my test grades were dropping. I was distracted, quiet, not myself.

I was, well, I was pregnant.

Seventeen-years-old, a "good" Christian girl in the Bible Belt South, and pregnant. It was, to put it mildly, less than ideal. I went to a large, diverse public high school where, to be perfectly honest, I thrived. Good grades, many friends, tons of extracurricular activities. I loved my school and the opportunities it provided me to grow not only as a student but also as a young woman trying to figure out how to achieve all of my hopes and dreams in college and beyond.

When I took a pregnancy test the day after I attended prom that year, suddenly what had been a world of possibilities for me the day before dwindled right before my eyes as they focused on that clearly positive pregnancy result. You see, at that time—and honestly, I'm not sure if it's any different now—pregnant students were not allowed to stay enrolled in my school.

Something about a distraction, I guess ...

There is no way I could ever really describe for you what those first few days and weeks were like for me. Unless you've been there yourself, you can never understand the fear. Fear of judgment, fear of punishment, fear of making the wrong decision. I was in complete agony. And yet, I knew I had to try and pull it together each day so as not to cause suspicion. But it was nearly impossible to make it through a day without crying.

So when this teacher, Mrs. Zee we'll call her, pulled me out into the hallway to check on me, I was terrified. If I close my eyes, I can still see myself propped against those lockers, arms crossed, looking at my shoes and wishing I was anywhere else in the world but there. I could have easily lied and told her I was just overwhelmed with school/parents/anything but the truth.

But I didn't lie. I knew nothing about her religious beliefs, her feelings about pregnant teenagers in school, or what sort of protocol the school's administration may have given her upon receiving information such as this. I just knew she genuinely seemed to care about my well-being, and I needed as much of that in my life at that moment as I could possibly get.

I don't remember the first thing she said to me, but I do remember her face. There wasn't a speck of judgment on it. Not one ounce of anything but love, and the acknowledgment of my pain as she hugged me. I remember she told me to be discreet with whom I told while I was making my decision because people loved to talk. I remember her telling me not to worry about the exam and to just do the best I could. I remember feeling in my heart of hearts that she was a safe space for me, and I was truly grateful.

She continued to be a champion of mine beyond that day in the hallway. She proved herself to be trustworthy, loving, and supportive through it all. And even after I had an emotional breakdown during the AP test and only scored a two out of five, thus not earning college credit, she assured me she was still proud. Proud that I showed up. Proud that I tried. Proud that I finished. I know it may sound silly to have been worried about a test when I obviously had MUCH bigger problems in my life, but honestly, the fact that she still kept me engaged and did everything she could to help me succeed was such an important gift she gave me each day.

And though I certainly didn't tell my son about this experience during our conversation, I couldn't help but hope that he too would have a teacher someday he trusted with his most personal of struggles. Obviously, my wish as his mother is that I can always be his safe space, but what I recognize now is that sometimes we are too close to the situation to be our children's "landing pad," so to speak. What this teacher did, and what so many others do on a daily basis, is provide a respite from the sometimes incredibly heavy struggles children face that even their closest friends and family don't know about.

I'm certain that Mrs. Zee had an opinion one way or the other about what I "should" do. Lord knows everyone else did. But as far as I can remember, she never pressed it upon me. She just kept on showing unconditional support. Something, by the way, ANY young woman in that situation truly needs.

Much is discussed about what the role of a teacher really is, and/or what it should be. I've been blessed with educators who went above and beyond merely teaching the curriculum in a syllabus in order to foster something bigger than a grade on a report card. I've had teachers who identified strengths and talents in me that helped shape the confidence I have in myself today. And I've had teachers who were just so damn in love with what they did that I couldn't help but love it too. But I don't think there could have been anything more valuable to me at that time than having a teacher who noticed I was struggling, took the time to find out why, and then held me up as I navigated my way through it.

This act came with no additional pay or recognition. It didn't earn her a special award or a write-up in the school newspaper. In fact, it very well could have landed her in the hot seat should the school find out. And yet, she did it anyway. That's the thing about great teachers, I suppose. They take risks for their students. They understand their influence on a student's life can last much longer than a school year's worth of lesson planning. Which is why, twenty years later, when I reflect upon all the teachers I've had in my life, she still rises to the top.

KELLY GREENWAY IS A TV PRODUCER AND AWARD-WINNING WRITER WHOSE ESSAYS HAVE BEEN FEATURED ON NUMEROUS SITES. SHE IS ALSO A CO-FOUNDER OF @MOMMYDEARESTINC, AN ONLINE COMMUNITY FOR MOTHERS SEEKING HUMOR AND HONESTY. SHE LOVES HER FAMILY, DARK CHOCOLATE, RED LIPSTICK, AND DISMANTLING THE PATRIARCHY.

17

But First They Cheered
By Galit Breen

I t's 1982.

I'm slumped in a heather-blue plastic student chair. The bottom is hard. The legs are shiny. My hand-me-down-clad arms encircle a smudged worksheet.

"You and you and you, come on over 'ere!" My teacher smiles as she gathers a group of children to her, pointing to each one with a cotton candy pink perfectly rounded nail. They gather to her side quickly, willingly, like magnets.

Their bright eyes, loud voices, and wide smiles surround me.

I was six-years-old and new to the States. I started the school year with four words in my repertoire: Yes. No. Mom. Dad.

My teacher, Mrs. McCrory, owned a southern drawl and this first-grade classroom in West Virginia.

She was vivid.

Impossibly full, white-blond hair.

Strong, frequent hugs.

Floral perfume.

Soft sweaters.

Pencil skirts.

On the first day of school she picked the phonetic spelling of my Hebrew name "G-a-l-i-t. Well that's just lovely, innint?" she drawled.

In the middle of the school year she pressed tattered copies of *Dick and Jane* into my mother's small hands saying, "Read these with 'er at home, mmkay?"

By the end of the school year, she squeezed me tightly and announced, "*Girl!* You're a reader!"

But on this day, many months earlier, we needed to tackle a worksheet.

Even though I was learning new words everyday—tree, flower, dog, cat—those grayish worksheets smeared with purple ink instantly had me slumping in my seat.

Biting my lip.

Running my hand through my hair.

And just ... sitting.

Because I had no idea what to do, where to write, how to start.

"Do ya see the E right here, honey? That E makes all the difference in the whole wide world," Mrs. McCrory says as she ushers that handful of children around my chair.

They lean on my desk, reaching across each other, and point to Mrs. McCrory's coveted E.

I glance down at my desk and can't help but take note of dirt under some fingernails and bright pink polish peeling off of the tips of others. I look up. Their serious faces and pronounced gestures are not lost on me.

A moment that feels like forever passes. I hear the bright white clock tick-tock-ing above me. The fluorescent school lights that fill every classroom I've ever been in form a spotlight around that moment-that-feels-like-forever.

Then, finally, one little boy's face lights up as he says, "You know! Like a grandpa has!"

He steps in front of the group, smile wide, and he wobbles, limps, and pretends to lean on a ...

"*Cane!*" I whisper, a smile that matches his slowly playing on my own lips.

I sit up quickly, pull my fingers out of my stick-straight hair, and place my pencil at the ready. I point to each letter with that school-sharp pencil point and say: c-a-n-e.

And they cheered.

They *cheered.*

And they patted me on the back. And they said things like, "Yes!" And, "You did it!" And, "Mrs. McCrory! She got *cane!*" making my victory ours.

But first and foremost, they cheered.

It's 1999.

I'm a classroom teacher in California. I face my kids, my students, sitting in a spinny, cushy, bright blue teacher chair.

There are fifteen languages spoken among the twenty-one of us. I'm one of four Caucasian people in the room. I'm in my element.

At circle time, I hold picture books in that one-handed, magical teacher way that ensures that everyone can see—and fall in love with —the page, while allowing me to point to the words, the pictures, the colors.

I point to each of these things relentlessly, just like Mrs. McCrory did for me.

They look up at me with eyes different shades of brown. Coffee. Caramel. Chocolate.

They call me Teacher.

They start on their bottoms, sitting "criss cross applesauce," but as the story continues, they edge closer and closer to each other, and to me.

In my spare time outside of class—the first year of teaching is brutal—I create learning buckets for them.

Small silver tin buckets filled with things that create meaning out of letters, numbers, and colors.

They're my version of Mrs. McCrory's *Dick and Jane* books and purple-smudged worksheets, and I fill every single nook and cranny of our classroom with them.

At work time, they gather around each others' desks.

They cheer for each other.

I squeeze them tight.

And by the end of the school year, they all respect the power of the letter E in the word "cane."

It's 2010.

I walk into my own daughter's first-grade classroom in Minnesota.

There's a shiny green apple on the wall with her name on it.

K-a-y-l-i it says in perfect kindergarten print; this is a skill I no longer possess.

Books line the walls. And the nooks. And the crannies.

The desks are pushed together in groups of four. Perfect for reaching across and leaning upon and pointing out important things, like the letter E.

I know that she will learn here.

As I run my index finger along Kayli's nameplate, a tall father walks by me.

His son fights sleep on his shoulder. "*Ssshh, esta bien.* It's okay." He pats his six-year-old's back.

"They just got back from Mexico last night at ten o'clock!" My daughter's teacher whispers loudly in my ear, touching my arm. Her years of experience shine through warm eyes. Her lipstick-edged smile is wide.

"Tell Mrs. Breen what you did this summer!" she addresses the sleepy boy. He smiles as he says, "Mexico. With all my cousins," never lifting his head off his father's strong shoulder.

"Now tell her in Spanish!" she says. And I know that he will learn here too.

Kayli leans into me and I hug her close, silently saying, "Cheer as loud as you can when he learns the word *cane*."

GALIT BREEN IS THE BESTSELLING AUTHOR OF *KINDNESS WINS, A SIMPLE GUIDE TO TEACHING YOUR CHILD TO BE KIND ONLINE*; THE TEDx TALK, "RAISING A DIGITAL KID WITHOUT HAVING BEEN ONE"; THE ONLINE COURSE RAISE YOUR DIGITAL KID™; AND THE FACEBOOK GROUP THE SAVVY PARENTS CLUB. SHE BELIEVES YOU CAN LET YOUR CHILD HAVE A PHONE AND STILL CREATE A GRASS-BENEATH-THEIR-BARE-FEET CHILD-HOOD FOR THEM. GALIT'S WRITING HAS BEEN FEATURED ON *THE HUFFIN-GTON POST, THE WASHINGTON POST,* BUZZFEED, *TIME,* AND MORE. SHE LIVES IN MINNESOTA WITH HER HUSBAND, THREE CHILDREN, AND A RIDICULOUSLY SPOILED MINI GOLDENDOODLE. FIND HER AT THESELIT-TLEWAVES.NET

18

I Teach Because I Have To

By Amber Leventry

"Y ou need to ask Ryan how he wants to start preschool. Does he want his peers and teachers to know him as a boy or as a girl? If Ryan wants to be seen as a girl, use the summer to switch pronouns and to get friends, family, and new teachers on board with the transition."

This was from Ryan's pediatrician in May 2016, about a month before Ryan turned three. My partner and I had scheduled the consultation because we had gone as far we could without using the word "transgender" to describe our child. We could no longer carry on using gender-neutral words to describe her, and we could no longer wonder if she simply wanted to be like her big sister. Our Ryan didn't want to wear clothes like big sis; she *was* a girl like big sis, and she wanted to wear clothes that affirmed her identity. Ryan was a girl. And she expected to start preschool as such.

Ryan, along with her twin brother, was assigned male at birth. The twins joined their two-mom, big-sister family as the baby bros.

For about eighteen months I was certain I had a daughter and two sons. But then one day while trying to get Ryan and her brother dressed to get outside so I didn't lose my stay-at-home-mom mind, Ryan began her process of creating uncertainty in my knowledge. She refused to put on a pair of navy sweatpants. It was not unusual for any of my kids to resist clothing, but there was something more adamant in her rejection of hand-me-down cotton.

She screamed and kept saying her big sister's name. I am not sure how I pieced it together, because an angry toddler with limited language is far from helpful, but it occurred to me that Ryan wanted to wear a pair of her big sister's leggings. I found the smallest pair we had in the house—a size four—and handed them to a size two-wearing Ryan. *Yes.* The grab, the smile, and the pride of wearing a pair of pink, blue, and purple-striped leggings with a hole in the knee told me I'd figured out what she'd wanted me to know. Ryan was about to teach us a lot of things.

Ryan has never said she is a boy. This is because she is a girl, but also because her other mama and I have never forced her to be anything other than who she is. Our daughter is transgender. But before she learned that word and before we introduced her to *I Am Jazz*, written by Jazz Jenning and Jessica Herthel, so she could see herself in a book, Ryan was simply a girl. Her boy body did not determine her gender identity, but the discrepancy between the two meant a label was needed so that I and the people in our lives could find ways to validate my child.

I identify as queer and nonbinary. I am both female and male. And, like my daughter, I was assigned a gender at birth that wasn't right. I, however, lived almost forty years with the female label. I was told I was a girl, so I lived as one. My heart falls in love with girls, but to see myself as a lesbian—a woman in love with another woman—feels wrong. I used the word "gay" to describe myself until I found that "queer" is the word that feels like home. It is a non-gendered way for me to describe my sexuality and identity.

I learned the word "nonbinary" a few years after the word "queer," and it took a few more years for me to embrace the term for myself. It wasn't that I wasn't nonbinary; it's that I didn't have the combination of language and confidence to "come out" as my true self.

No one should ever feel like they have to come out when their identity is somewhere on the LGBTQIA+ spectrum, but until society learns that anything not defined as heterosexual and cisgender is in fact normal and worth respecting, we are obligated to "come out." But coming out is a superficial act required of us because we live in a society in which any deviation from the norm requires an explanation. We already know who we are, yet we make announcements so we can live a life of authenticity. We come out so we can educate others of our differences. We come out because it's lonely to live in the shadows of our truth.

My daughter never came out to us because we never made her feel like she had to be anything based on her genitalia. But the fact that she is transgender forced me to come out as her biggest advocate. If I wanted to make the world a safer and kinder place for her to live, I needed to be a louder speaker and a more patient teacher.

I am not a perfect teacher, but I am a good one. I am also a tired one who is constantly learning.

Educating schools, workplaces, and communities feels like a one-person-at-a-time gig when it comes to LGBTQIA+ topics. These topics are taboo, misunderstood, and rejected. The level of comfort when it comes to talking about gay people, transgender folks, and nonbinary individuals varies among people as greatly as weather varies between states on a day in April. It can be sunny and eighty in some places and snowy and thirty in others. Some people are accepting and affirming; others are hateful and dangerous to my existence. A lot of people are in the middle—cloudy and cool.

I cannot expect to affect change by presenting one universal explanation of what it means to be queer, transgender, or nonbinary. I need to learn individual biases, upbringings, and knowledge before I can move the needle toward understanding and acceptance. I am not pushing an agenda despite being accused of doing so. I am trying to find common ground while sharing my lived experiences and the experiences of other queer people to help the heteronormative world see me and my daughter as humans who deserve respect and equal rights.

The world is an ugly and scary place for LGBTQIA+ people. This is something I have learned. I have also learned how exhausting and heavy that knowledge can be when it becomes your life's work to make it less ugly and less scary. As an advocate and public figure, I receive a lot of pushback, hate mail, and threats to my life. It makes me wonder if I am making any changes. It makes me wonder if I will always have to fight to be seen. It makes me wonder if my daughter will be able to live a life without the depression, anxiety, shame, and fear that has accompanied my journey.

Then I get a message from someone who tells me they are going to start using more inclusive language because it is the right thing to do. I get an email from someone thanking me for paving the way for their nonbinary child. I get notes from parents thanking me for helping them understand their own transgender child. I am sent pictures of LGBTQIA+ themed books that parents have put into the hands of their kids, placed on shelves in their local library, or purchased for their child's classroom.

These are not just reminders of the good work that I am doing; they are the fuel I need to keep going.

When a contact emails me to tell me one of the classes I am teaching on LGBTQIA+ topics is full, I know my work is needed. I know people are as ready to learn as I am to teach. The next step is to deliver my message in the most powerful, palatable, and meaningful way. People will show up to learn, and I will show up to teach. But this dynamic is only as good as the willingness between my audience and me to be vulnerable. The best way to hear and deliver a message is when all walls are down.

Ryan's walls were never up, and I hope they will never have to be. My walls are slowly starting to crumble, and I am using the rubble as material to build something better.

I am nonbinary, both male and female, and want to be seen as such. I want my pronouns respected and to be included in conversations without gendered language.

Ryan is transgender, all girl, and wants to be seen as such. She only knows a life of being respected and included in conversations with language that affirms her gender.

We know ourselves better than anyone else despite what others think they know about gender, sex, and sexuality. It is not my job to justify my or my daughter's existence. And it is not her job to educate others. I have, however, decided to make it my life's mission to teach.

People have the capacity to learn and understand if they are willing to open their hearts and minds. That ability offers a gift so many others take for granted: to simply live our lives. I just want to make it through the day without the constant reminder of my differences. My daughter just wants to be a kid.

My daughter refused to put on navy sweat pants. She refused to wear a label that didn't fit.

Her simple act of defiance began a chain reaction of education and learning. I am learning the best ways to help my daughter become the person she was always meant to be. I quickly learned that I needed to teach others how to do the same; no one else can support her the way I can. I am learning the best way to also advocate for myself comes in seeing the potential for everyone to be a student and in the potential for me to be able to teach them something.

AMBER LEVENTRY IS A QUEER, NONBINARY WRITER AND ADVOCATE. THEY LIVE IN VERMONT AND HAVE THREE KIDS, INCLUDING TWINS AND A TRANSGENDER DAUGHTER. AMBER'S WRITING APPEARS ON *THE WASHINGTON POST*, RAVISHLY, GROWN AND FLOWN, LONGREADS, THE NEXT FAMILY, AND SAMMICHES & PSYCH MEDS. THEY ARE A STAFF WRITER FOR SCARY MOMMY. THEY ALSO RUN FAMILY RHETORIC BY AMBER LEVENTRY, A FACEBOOK PAGE DEVOTED TO ADVOCATING FOR LGBTQ FAMILIES ONE STORY AT A TIME.

AMBER WORKS WITH SCHOOLS TO MAKE CURRICULUM LGBTQ

INCLUSIVE AND AFFIRMING AND HAVE SPOKEN ON PANELS AND TAUGHT WORKSHOPS TO HELP PEOPLE BECOME BETTER INFORMED ALLIES.

FOLLOW THEM ON TWITTER AND INSTAGRAM @AMBERLEVENTRY. AND VISIT THEIR WEBSITE TO HIRE THEM FOR SPEAKING ENGAGEMENTS AND LGBTQ TRAINING SESSIONS.

19

Pregame Pep Talk
By Meredith Napolitano

Breathe.

Seriously. Deep breaths. You can do this; you just need to prepare yourself.

They can't actually *do* anything to you. I mean, they might hurt your feelings. Maybe challenge your intelligence a little. And your parenting skills. Maybe take an event that's supposed to be fun and make it feel more like a performance review. They might make you might want to chug a glass of wine and scream in the car later. But they can't *really* do anything. It'll be fine.

You can do this.

Honestly, they're *just* people. It'll be easy. And you are a strong, confident woman. You are HAPPY with your life choices. They don't have power over you.

You can do this.

You can bring your homeschooled kids to this family party.

I mean, these people *love* you! And they love your kids! They're just interested in your life! They are nothing like the cashier at Panera who went from chatting happily about the *People* magazine cover on this season's *The Bachelor* to looking grave, and *apparently* harboring both knowledge and passion for child development and how amazing public education is these days when she realized your homeschooled kids were with you for lunch *in the middle of a school day.* Because there's nothing like switching topics from broccoli cheddar soup and thirty women looking for love to the nuances of Common Core math and socialization and what that might mean in your children's overall emotional growth. It wasn't weird at all to talk through your curriculum for her approval while ordering an iced green tea. Then watch her suspiciously eye the kids for signs of ... umm ... not exactly sure what, while they ate grilled cheese and got an insane amount of cookie crumbs on the floor.

But you *did* it. You answered ALL her questions politely. See? You are totally capable. And you only had minor anxiety in the car that she was secretly writing down your license plate number and planning to call the Department of Education on you.

Okay, so let's be proactive here. Let's prepare. There can't be that much to worry about.

First things first. This time, for *sure,* you are going to make *certain* your kids know what grade they are in.

God, last time was embarrassing. I mean, come on, kid, I know your math book and your reading book and your science book all say different things. But we took a picture for Facebook back in September that said FIRST DAY OF THIRD GRADE, so that's what we're sticking with!

Okay, so you'll role play that one before we head out. This one is in first grade, this one is in third. Mental note to make girls memorize that.

Once you pass that barrier, you'll get the inevitable legal questioning and social skills inquisition, intended to catch you out on our questionable life and make you realize the error of your ways. Even though you aren't hiding anything, and the girls are already happily playing with their cousins and chatting with the adults, you'll still have to go through that. Let's be real here, you know that's not up for debate. So let's get all your snarky answers out of the way now, in your head, so you can smile and respond politely later.

You're still homeschooling? Is that legal?

Nope. We're deep undercover. Except for you. And everyone listening to us now. And I keep forgetting and going out in public and then posting about it online DURING SCHOOL HOURS. But we still haven't been caught, so shhh! Don't tell!

What are you doing for socialization?

Ugh, socialization is totally overrated. I'm teaching them how to avoid human interaction.

Aren't you worried about how they'll live in the real world?

Ummm ... aren't we in the real world now?

How will they learn to deal with bullies?

Girls! Come here! I want you to watch how I deal with a bully! Ooh! Would you also like to harass them so I can show them how to file a report to human resources? I mean, life skills, right?

Do they have ANY friends? HOW?

Gee, I can't imagine WHERE anyone would manage to meet friends outside of a school setting. Certainly not dance or soccer or Girl Scouts or co-op classes or the pool. That's why I haven't formed a single bond with another person since graduation. Once you're out of school, that's it.

Don't they want to go to REAL SCHOOL?

Is real school located in the same place as the real world? No wonder we're having such troubles. Apparently we can't find that place and we will keep going to pretend school in the pretend world.

No, no, don't say anything like that. Get it all out now. Last time, you really insulted your cousin's mother in law's friend, and she got PISSED, which meant your cousin's mother in law had to hear it, which means your cousin had to hear it, which means YOU had to hear about how rude you are to people who are JUST TRYING TO LOOK OUT FOR YOUR POOR KIDS and how your cousin's mother in law's friend is certainly NEVER going to make the mistake of trying to be nice to ANYONE again. Then your cousin will call and vent to your aunt because she doesn't have time for this nonsense, and your aunt will call YOUR mom and you'll get another inquisition from your mom about how she can't believe you insulted...wait, who did you insult?

Okay, so you know these questions are coming, so you need to just smile and give the same answers that you always do, like you're reading from a pamphlet called "Super Polite Answers to Give When People Ask You About Socialization at First Communion Parties."

Side note: You should totally write that pamphlet. There's definitely a market for it.

If you pass the socialization hurdle, you know you aren't done, so be prepared to discuss the nuances of your curriculum.

Are you ready to list your subjects? The specific book you're using for each one? What you have covered, are currently covering, and plan to cover before the end of the year? Where did you find all these? Does your school district know what you're "up to?" Do your kids have desks? What? They don't? Well then, WHERE DO THEY DO THEIR WORK? Do you give them tests? Do you FAIL THEM?

Keep smiling, keep answering. Now you can toss out those buzz words like "individualized education" and "actual learning time" and "proven effective strategies throughout the world" and "formative assessments" and studies about unstructured play time. Discuss with passion what impacted your decision to switch math curriculum, and why you decided to go with traditional spelling rather than solely focusing on word study. Name drop, name drop, name drop. Now, they won't know any of these names, but this DOES NOT MATTER. Keep name dropping. You might be asked about your educational credentials. I know, we discussed how you were a public school teacher last year at that baptism, and you even earned a sigh of relief and even a hint of a pass, but that does NOT mean you are exempt from the same discussion this year.

If you get through that, you've passed the second hurdle. You sure *sound* like you might know what you're doing. Well, maybe. But you won't *really* know that until they chat with your kids and size *them* up.

And don't forget, this might not happen until much later! You'll probably feel successful after your curriculum talk, and you'll walk away with a smile and get yourself a celebratory glass of wine and maybe even snag what's left on the plate of cheese. But, *ugh*, remember Thanksgiving? You got the whole inquisition done before dinner, and were able to go back to chatting with your cousin about *America's Got Talent*. During dinner you heard all about that home renovation and everyone agreed that renovations are the worst, but that the new kitchen was totally worth it. And then everyone talked about Black Friday sales as you helped clean up the kitchen, and it wasn't until you were eating pumpkin pie and drinking coffee when the mandatory pop quiz started. And you were kicking yourself because your kids were inhaling cupcakes and didn't give one single crap about math facts or irregular verb tenses or state capitals. And then the smug smiles started, even though the other kids at the table weren't exactly jumping in with the answers. This is not about those kids. Those kids go to "real school." Those kids are normal, despite the frosting on their noses, and they don't need your grandmother's next-door neighbor to quiz them. They've got standardized tests for that. Don't be silly.

But *your* kids need someone looking out for them, and Mrs. Next Door used to substitute when her kids were small, so she knows things and she's well up to the task. She will take this duty very seriously, so don't forget to prepare the kids. Start with reminding them that "number bonds" is basically another way of referring to adding and subtracting, so they DO SO know what they are. And that "writer's workshop" is pretty similar to the writing we do, so if they ask your kids what they do during writer's workshop, they are not allowed to say "we don't do that." Hey, think of it as your days as a public school teacher (remember that?) and do some good old test prep. And your third grader is plenty old enough for the fine art of BS and faking it. If you sell it right, you can hint that this sign of maturity, in the form of extolling why exactly science is her favorite subject, might mean a pair of high heels for the next dress up occasion, and she'll probably do you proud.

Okay, so let's see. What are the perennial questions you always get? Right! Work on multiplication facts. Especially the sixes, sevens, and eights. People LOVE to quiz homeschooled kids on those tables. Oh, and pick a couple of obscure, impressive sounding words and spend the next week learning how to spell them. Ooh, and also, don't forget to practice sample dialogue and what the subjects are called, so when your six-year-old, who has been fascinated with learning the presidents in order, is asked what she's learning about in history, she doesn't stare at the questioner with blank eyes and say that otters are her favorite animal.

Oh, and make sure they can each list at LEAST two unique friends, with backgrounds on how they met, how often they see each other, and what they like to do together. Bonus points for listing both a homeschooled friend AND a non-homeschooled friend.

Two to three extracurriculars too. Good, social, mainstream ones.

Oh, and make sure they've got a good list of favorite books. Classic books. This is no place to share your love of finding new authors. That may all be well and good, but they did NOT get those books from a school, so their value can't yet be determined.

If you want to avoid the smug side-eye, you need to make sure these kids bring their A game. A dessert table is no excuse for distraction and vague answers. These kids need to BACK YOU UP.

See! You've got this! You got grade level, socialization, curriculum, test prep...oh crap. What if they go deep and try to understand WHY you're homeschooling? You'll end up being asked about vaccines and religion and politics and somehow the fact that you feel like you're actually pretty middle of the road and normal and do ONE THING off the beaten path will work against you. So you'll say... you'll say...

Wow. This is getting to be a lot to prepare. And given your stuttering during the Panera encounter, you are a much more effective conversationalist in the shower, or when you're alone in the car, and not when you're wishing that your nephew didn't need quite so many godparents to attend this thing and why the spotlight always needs to be on you and not your younger brother, *who,* by the way, is totally changing jobs *again.*

Oh, forget it. Just smile and remember the important stuff.

You're still at it. You still love it. And even though you have those days when you fantasize about dropping the girls off and sitting ALONE, all day long, and you also have those days when you want to bang your head into the kitchen table and beg someone else to get them to finish their writing, those days don't happen all that much. And despite society's abnormal level of interest in what you do every day, you honestly wouldn't have it any other way. You get to be a mom, a teacher, and a normal, somewhat socially awkward woman all at once, and that's worth whatever anyone may throw at you.

MEREDITH NAPOLITANO IS A FORMER TEACHER AND PERFORMER AND A CURRENT WEARER OF MANY LABELS, INCLUDING MOM, HOME-SCHOOLING MOM, DANCE MOM, SOCCER MOM, SUBPAR HOUSEKEEPER, AND PART-TIME WRITER. SHE EXPLORES ALL THESE LABELS ON HER BLOG, FROM MEREDITH TO MOMMY. MEREDITH LIVES IN CONNECTICUT WITH HER FAMILY. HER WRITING HAS BEEN FEATURED ON A VARIETY OF WEBSITES AND IN SEVERAL PUBLISHED ANTHOLOGIES, BUT SHE IS AT HER WITTIEST IN TEXT MESSAGES.

20

Gifts from the Heart
By Courtney Fitzgerald-Stevens

"Why did you become a teacher?" is a question I have been asked a million times. The simple answer is, "I became a teacher because of a hug." This answer, that is one hundred percent true, is often met with eye rolling and disbelief. College prepared me for many aspects of teaching: how to write lesson plans; how to teach kids to read; how to build number sense; and how to arrange a room to maximize student learning. I studied behavior theories, discipline models, and have read countless books by educational experts. Becoming a certified teacher was one of the easiest things I have done in my life. Actually teaching? I don't think anything other than experience prepares the excited college student for that roller coaster ride. I definitely was not prepared for the countless stories of sadness or touching moments that being a teacher actually brings into my heart.

When I started my career, holidays like Halloween and Valentine's Day meant treats, class parties, and the occasional gift. Two states, three districts, and sixteen years later, the structure of school days are quite different. One thing that has remained the same are the precious gifts that students give.

Throughout the years, I have learned that no one gives gifts as well as elementary school children. Some of my students have been able to buy me gifts from a store like a gift card, lotion, or bookmark. They might give me a six-pack of my favorite diet soda, a bag of coffee, a memory card for my camera, or some other trinket that screamed, "Hey, I listen to your stories and I know things about you!" Every year, I have at least one student who travels to his/her home country and brings me back a coin purse, paperweight, or candy.

Of course, with teaching comes the standard, yet useful gifts like coffee mugs, tree decorations, school supplies, books, and chocolate. Boys often say, "My mom bought this for you," not realizing that the card they signed that morning, meant that the gift was actually from them. Recently, I was given free-range fresh eggs and it made my day. One of the most unforgettable gifts was a silk rose from a third grader. It was beautiful, however, at home it came apart and was actually silk underwear.

I have had numerous students who gave me items from their houses because they could not afford to buy a gift. Sometimes it's a necklace made out of worn-out glow sticks, a school picture, or a homemade card with countless misspellings. Students have handed me smelly stuffed animals that I absolutely do not want to touch, as I am afraid of what creature might live in it. I have received art projects and homemade magnets. Once, a student gave me her mom's diamond ring that she stole off the nightstand. Another time, a student made me a card out of every homework pass he earned in third grade but did not use because math was too much fun to miss.

I will never forget my first year teaching third grade. I had a student who absolutely LOVED holidays. She put tallies on her desk to count down until the holiday. Nothing stopped her from writing on her desk, not even having to clean the classroom during recess. I learned on Valentine's Day why she was so excited: this child absolutely loved to give gifts. I can still see her heart sweater, pink skirt, and heart-printed tights she wore that Valentine's Day. She was smiling as she carried in a shiny purple gift bag with pink tissue paper.

"I brought this for you, Mrs. Fitzgerald. I hope you LOVE it!" As a new teacher who had not yet mastered the awkwardness of opening gifts in front of expectant children, I peeked inside the bag. I saw a pile of dirt, a plastic pot, and a trampled flower. As I carefully took it out, dirt spilled all over the day's lesson plans, my desk, my skirt, and the floor. The pink flowers looked like they had seen better days, but none of that fazed my student. "I hope you love flowers!" I learned from a couple of my students that she dropped the gift bag down the stairs as she came into the building that morning. However, that was a distant memory to this sweetie who was excited to give me a gift.

Later that year, I had a student transfer in who spent most of her school year sleeping on various couches, living with numerous relatives, and attending multiple schools. Poverty and homelessness can harden children and affect how they feel about a stable adult in their lives. On the last day of school, this student, who had been in my room for less than two months, brought in a dolphin statue. Part of the plastic was missing, the paint had worn off in many places. She held it in her hand, as she came up to my desk that warm June morning.

"I bought this at the dollar store. It was only a dollar." She stared at me, blinking her eyes.

"Oh, it is beautiful! What a neat thing to buy at the dollar store!" I exclaimed, not sure what to say.

She walked away, set the dolphin statue on her desk. Right before recess, she brought it back to me. "Mrs. Fitzgerald, if you want it, you can have it. It was only a dollar. I got it at the dollar store with my money."

"Oh, you are so sweet! If you want to give it to me, I would love it. But if you want to keep it, I want you to have it." She stared at me, without saying a word, walked away and took the dolphin statue out to recess.

Before school let out for the year, she brought the dolphin statue to me again. "You can have it if you want it. It was only a dollar. I got it at the dollar store." This time, I said, "Thank you. I love it." She handed it to me, gave me a hug, and walked out of my life.

No one gives gifts as well as elementary school children. Whether I am handed a beautifully wrapped package with a store-bought gift, a school picture, or something that was made from items found/stolen from the home, I know that the package is not just an item, but a piece of a child who will forever be in my heart.

COURTNEY FITZGERALD-STEVENS IS A WIDOW, WIFE, MOM, STEPMOM, TEACHER, WRITER, AND DREAMER. SHE WRITES ABOUT HER PERFECTLY IMPERFECT LIFE AT OURSMALLMOMENTS.COM. SHE IS BEST KNOWN FOR HER VIRAL PIECE CALLED "YOU WENT TO A FUNERAL AND THEN YOU WENT HOME." SHE CAN BE FOUND AROUND THE INTERNET, INCLUDING TWO ANTHOLOGIES.

21

Basket of Cheer—The Kindness of Montessori Teachers
By Kris Amels

My daughter, Izzy, had attended the same little local Montessori school for a year and a half when we discovered she needed more surgery to correct her hip dysplasia. Because she'd spend a few months in a body cast (called a spica) afterward to keep her hip in place, Iz wouldn't be able to attend the tiny school, which lacked wheelchair access. It was with a heavy heart that I told the school's owner, Miss H., about Izzy's upcoming surgery and why she'd have to drop out of school. The surgery was scheduled for March, so she'd miss the last 4 months. Miss H. was understanding and supportive, and immediately asked me if there was anything she could do to help Izzy. Overwhelmed, I said I couldn't think of anything.

On Iz's last day of school, the four teachers, Miss H., Miss M., Miss A., and Miss D., gathered around Izzy for goodbye hugs and presented her with a basket almost as tall as she was filled with little toys, Montessori lessons, and things to color. There were books to read and a penmanship tablet for practice. Tucked in front was a tiny felt tic-tac-toe board with pink and blue tulip shapes that Iz still plays with, more than three years later. Every single item had been chosen with an immobilized child in mind: all supported fine-motor skill development, and all aligned with things Iz liked to do. It was the most thoughtful thing anyone has ever done for her. The teachers lined up to see Iz off that last day, and tears sparkled in our eyes as we hugged goodbye.

The surgery went well but the hospital stay was grueling; four days of Izzy screaming in pain from unrelenting, brutally painful muscle spasms. She doesn't remember all of it; most of what she can recall is having the hospital's therapy rabbit, Clovis, visit her and sit on her cast while she brushed his soft brown fur over and over. The stress of being unable to stop her pain, even though I was with her the entire time, turned my hair almost completely white. It was really, really rough. But we made it through, made it home, and started the long and sometimes lonely process of healing. So, it was a most welcome surprise when Miss H. called and invited Izzy back to school to celebrate her birthday in April.

Montessori birthdays are a big deal. The kid who's celebrating gets to hold a bright blue globe and walk in a circle around a little lit candle in a bowl on the floor that represents the sun. Radiating from the sun are slips of paper with the months printed on them. The kid starts at their birthday month and walks around the circle the same number of times as their new age, ending up at their birthday month. This illustrates the trip the earth makes around the sun, and that a year has passed since the child's last birthday. Because Iz was turning four, they'd go around the circle four times. It's adorable.

My husband and Miss M. carried Izzy in her wheelchair up the steps to the school on her birthday. The kids were delighted to see each other, and they argued about who would be the lucky friends who could sit next to the birthday girl for cookies. Miss M. pushed Iz around the circle, explaining that her sister was also in a wheelchair, and so she was a pro at driving a chair. Izzy was so happy to see her schoolmates again, who were curious about the cast and the wheel-chair. Some of the kids knocked on Iz's cast while she laughed. Miss H. stood, smiling, off to the side with us, watching as the kids enjoyed themselves. Iz finally parked at a little table, set with colorful napkins and cookies, and shared a treat with her schoolmates.

I'll always be grateful for this beautiful act of kindness Miss H. showed Izzy. She made sure Iz wouldn't miss her birthday journey and could spend some social time with her friends. That big basket of toys and books kept Iz busy for months. Miss H. may have taught kindness in her Montessori school, but she embodied it in real life.

We had tears sparkling in our eyes again that day as we left, but these were tears of happiness.

KRIS AMELS IS A FABULOUSLY FRAZZLED FRAU, EX-REFORM SCHOOL KID, MOM, WIFE, WRITER, AND A FULL-TIME COLLEGE STUDENT. SHE'S FIFTY YEARS OLD AND HAS A SEVEN-YEAR-OLD KID, IZZY, WHO IS GENER-ALLY HILARIOUS. BOTH MOM AND DAUGHTER HAVE HIP DYSPLASIA, BUT IT'S COOL; THEY ROCK IT. KRIS BLOGS AT WHY MOMMY BLOG AND YOU CAN FIND HER ON FACEBOOK.

22

What I Make
By Abby Byrd

They pushed me too far.

All year, I had been trying to get these eighth-graders to care about something outside of themselves, or at least care about what would come next in their lives, which they blithely ignored. They weren't kids who had been beaten down by poverty—far from it. Most of them had wealthy parents. They wore the right clothes and the right shoes.

They had no reason to look at me the way they looked at me.

Why it matters was my last tack. "You don't think any of this matters?" I asked, raising my voice. "What do you think is going to happen when you leave here? What do you think you're going to accomplish?" My question was met with indifference, some snickers, a few eye rolls, and a smirk from Matt. I started to shake and get louder. "What exactly is it you plan to do that you think you won't have to do any work or follow any rules? Because if you don't change, you're gonna be at Taco Bell making chalupas."

I knew I had crossed a line. It was my fourth year teaching, and I'd certainly made mistakes, but I'd never said anything so unprofessional in the classroom. With that comment, I had set the tone for what was to follow.

"I'd rather work at Taco Bell than be a teacher," responded Matt, the smirker. "You guys make sucky money."

Kids laughed. At least half the class. I felt a flash of something, but I still don't know if it was anger or pain or both. I'd given them everything I had to give, and that's what they thought? The two degrees I'd earned, the hours I'd spent planning lessons and reading their words—listening to them from the page, talking back to them in purple ink—all of that was worth nothing to them?

"Get out of my room," I said as calmly as I could. He took his time leaving, still smirking, while some of his cronies laughed. That was when I started to cry as I yelled. "I can't believe you're laughing at him! He is an idiot!" A second line crossed: You never, under any circumstances, call a student a name. What had I done? I was sure to be reprimanded, maybe even fired. I had crossed yet another line by losing control of my emotions and crying in front of students.

I walked from the front of the classroom to my desk, where I sat down and put my head in my hands. In the two minutes that were left before the lunch bell, kids chatted and laughed as if nothing had happened. Michael, who consistently spelled his own name wrong, ranted to no one in particular: "She can't tell me what I'm gonna be. I'm gonna be a pro football player!"

Once the kids had filed out, I sobbed at my desk. My first impulse was to flee. I looked around at the items on my desk and decided I could do without all of it. I would take just my wallet and keys and start driving, putting as many miles as possible between me and this intolerable feeling of worthlessness. Obviously, I had been wasting my talents. What had I achieved? I was *just* a teacher.

I was out of my chair and reaching for my purse—that close to leaving—when Zelia from sixth period walked in. She wanted to know if she could leave her books there over lunch.

"Of course," I said, sitting back down and trying to hide my tears.

"Oh, Ms. Byrd." She rushed up to me. "You have been crying."

"I'm sorry. I-it wasn't a good class, that's all."

"Well, whatever it is, I know it will all be better. I am sure, okay? You will be all right." She smiled brightly.

I swallowed hard when Zelia went to lunch. If I walked out, she would come back in twenty-five minutes and find that I had abandoned her. So would Cory. And Sarah. And Albert. Albert, who alone would have been enough reason for me to stay.

Albert was a lanky, hunched Chinese kid who hadn't spoken a word the whole first month. His face was always expressionless. He had taped his broken eyeglasses together with Scotch tape, and all of his pants and shirts were too short for his gangly limbs. He never did homework. When I badgered him for the first assignment of the year, he kept his eyes down. He would only nod in reply to whatever I said. It became a challenge for me to try to crack him.

One day at the end of class, as I walked by his desk, I noticed him studying a piece of piano music and asked him if he played. I told him that I too played, and we had our first conversation—albeit stilted, and without eye contact on his part. I learned that his recital was coming up, so I pressed a bit more and found out when and where. "Can I come?" I asked, hoping I hadn't pushed too far. He shrugged. I took that as a "yes."

A few nights later in an elementary school cafeteria, I watched the most mysterious and amazing student I had ever met play Ellmenreich's "Spinning Song"—and I was smiling, because that song had once been my recital song. I remembered its steady pattern of eighth notes on the bass. Albert attacked the piano. He had memorized the whole piece, and hammered it out, yet there was no musicality to his playing—no dynamics, no emotion.

After meeting Albert's piano teacher, I understood why. "Albert doesn't have a piano, you know," she confided. "So it's very difficult for him. The only time he gets to play on a piano is here, at lessons."

That's when I learned that Albert had been studying piano for almost five years on a Casio keyboard with only four octaves. The next day, still in disbelief, I sent out a staff-wide email asking if anyone knew where to get a cheap piano. A science teacher had one in her attic; I had the money to pay movers. Within two weeks, Albert had a piano.

The next time I attended one of Albert's recitals, I was astounded by the change in his technique. He had learned what the keys felt like and how to strike them. He no longer attacked the instrument; he played it. He had become, I realized with some chagrin, a much, much better pianist than I was at his age.

I noticed changes in the classroom too. By the end of second quarter, I was finally getting Albert to turn in some work. He started earning 100% on vocabulary quizzes, and I figured out that this seemingly apathetic child was easily the smartest kid in the class. I let him and several other students split off from the group and read *Animal Farm*, which I was teaching to my GT classes. At lunch, I invited those few students into my room to watch the movie. The funny parts made Albert smile—the first time I ever saw him smile.

I wasn't thinking about all this as I sat crying at my desk. I only knew that even though I wanted so badly to flee, to drive home and cry some more and then go off to become a barista or a sushi chef or a performer in Vegas, I couldn't. I could not leave knowing that Albert would walk into my class the next day and find that I had abandoned him.

I gutted through the afternoon classes, through the rest of the year. But I put emotional distance between teaching and myself. I told myself I was superior to it. I resolved to take the GRE and pursue a graduate degree in English. I would once again embrace academia, where I'd receive perpetual validation of my worth: a neat series of As at the end of every quarter.

My plan to take refuge in academia didn't work out, largely because the math section of the GRE is terrifying. But by the end of that year, I had realized I was meant for the far more complicated endeavor of teaching. I had always assumed that my former teachers expected more of me, that they'd be dismayed to find that I'd become "just" a teacher. But when I began to unpack those feelings, they didn't make sense. My affection for my own students was unconditional, not based on their achievements. So why wouldn't my teachers feel the same way about me? Why had I assumed that they'd see me as a failure? Teaching requires not only intellect, but also creativity, patience, resilience, and compassion. My own teachers had probably recognized those gifts in me, which was why, when I'd contacted my favorite teacher during my first year, she'd said, "I am not at all surprised that you're a teacher." At the time, I didn't know what she meant. I even wondered if she'd insulted me somehow. Had she meant that I chose the easiest option? Or more important, because it was the best option available to someone whose parents had grown up poor?

It would take me almost another two decades of teaching to realize that I had been seeing the world through working-class goggles. Succeeding in school, to me, was the highest good, because that was the way up. That was—although I never understood this consciously—the way to elevate oneself above those who worked for minimum wage. What message, exactly, had I been trying to send my students when I admonished them that their academic failings would lead to a job at Taco Bell? I had been trying to shame them, and in doing so, I shamed my grandparents, who worked in factories. My mother, who spent my middle school years working in a convenience store. The shame was on me. I deserved to be cut by smirking Matt's remark.

As much as I tried to escape from the working class, I scorned the ones above me, those who were lucky enough to be born into privilege and had done nothing to earn it. I hated the thought that my students would coast through school and be taken care of financially by their parents regardless of their achievements. In fact, I don't know why I chose "working at Taco Bell" over "being handed everything by your parents." I guess instead of attacking the students' own ethos it was easier to bait them with people for whom we could share contempt.

Whenever I interact with students now, I'm always careful to let them know that they matter to me, regardless of what they are or are not achieving. The last time I saw Albert, at his senior recital, I approached him afterward and shook his hand, as I always did. I usually said, "Congratulations," and perhaps we chatted superficially about what classical music he was listening to or what he'd like to learn to play next. But this time, I needed to say something more.

"I am very proud of you," I began. "But I want you to know that I always will be, even if you stopped playing the piano tomorrow."

Staring at the floor, he smiled a little.

After teaching at the school where I met Albert for one year, I accepted a position at a private school, swearing I'd never teach in public school again. Eventually, I did go back to teach in two excellent public schools, working largely with highly motivated students. I still have frustrating days when I think things might be better behind an espresso machine or a sushi bar or onstage in a Vegas hotel. I still have days when I'm haunted by the specter of my own expectations. But most of the time I'm grateful that I can spend my life doing something meaningful. A teaching career is like a love affair that has torn out your heart: You wouldn't change any of it. You'd do it all again. It's not that you've forgotten the constant frustration and occasional humiliation; you remember. But the beautiful moments win. The beautiful moments render the painful moments powerless.

Teacher and poet Taylor Mali has a brilliant poem called "What Teachers Make." It's his response to a rude dinner party guest who scoffs at his career choice and asks condescendingly about his salary. At the end of the poem, Mali fires back, "I make a goddamn difference. What do *you* make?"

Sometimes I think about Matt, the smirker who brought me to tears that day. I confess to wondering now that he's in his early thirties what he's doing with his life. Which storyline, out of the myriad storylines I've constructed for him in my imagination, is real? How much money does he make? In my mind, he's a sort of Schrodinger's cat, at the same time obscenely wealthy and abjectly poor. Whatever is actually in the box is irrelevant. I already know the only thing I need to know: I can live on what I make.

ABBY BYRD's WORK HAS APPEARED ON *THE HUFFINGTON POST* AND SCARY MOMMY, AMONG OTHER SITES, AND IN SEVERAL ANTHOLOGIES. SHE RUNS THE BLOG LITTLE MISS PERFECT AT ABBYTHEWRITER.COM—A TROVE OF EXISTENTIAL ANGST, BITING HUMOR, AND BILE. HUNDREDS OF CLOWNS ONCE PRAYED FOR HER EN MASSE; CLEARLY, THEY ACHIEVED NOTHING. CONNECT WITH ABBY ON FACEBOOK AND GOODREADS.

23

All You Need Is Love and Number 2 Pencils
By Stacey Waltzer

The music teacher pushed past me on her way out of my classroom door. She mumbled something to herself but I couldn't make it out. I walked into a room full of five-year-olds who had just barely started kindergarten. Taking a deep breath, I asked what happened. The quietest kid got up and placed something in my hand. I slowly looked down to see a teeny tiny baby tooth with just a bit of blood on it. It was enough to make this beginning teacher's stomach lurch. The loudest kid in the class then took the opportunity to announce that he was the one who had pulled his friend's tooth out for him. The class waited to see my reaction. Their eyes got really big. I asked him why he would pull another kid's tooth out. His response? The kid was annoying him by wiggling it the ENTIRE TIME they had music. Then he nonchalantly began playing with a pile of pencils that were on his desk.

College classes do not prepare you for these moments. The professors are too busy teaching you where to find that perfect picture book or how to use manipulatives for math. Writing the perfect lesson plan is another big focus when you are studying to be a teacher. Little do you know, the plan never turns out the way it is intended to be.

It's not all about the pencils and the books either.

My teaching career began in 2001 in a New York City elementary school. My job was to teach math to kids in grades K-5. Then on the morning of September 11, everything changed in ways we did not see coming.

There was a first-grade class who did not have the best reputation for being model students. Although they were very smart, these kids could give even the most experienced teacher a run for their money with regards to behavior management. Their teacher came in that morning before the Towers fell and packed everything up. She quit. There was no notice. The administration put me in that room to cover the class through the rest of the day. I remember parents picking their kids up early as the entire city and country tried to make sense out of the terrible tragedy. Two weeks later, this class officially became mine as I was named their new first-grade teacher. The behaviors in that room escalated. There was a girl who cried all the time, and another student who put on her coat and threatened to leave in the middle of the day. One boy would slither his way under all the desks while I was teaching. I am also pretty sure that one kid did throw a pencil at my head. The kids were loud and uncooperative. I wasn't sure where to start.

I cried every day in the school bathroom.

Eventually through support staff, we learned that a few of the kids in my class were convinced something was going to happen to me if they got too attached. Through conversations we learned that many of them saw their teacher quit the morning of 9/11. Because of this, they were convinced when she didn't come back that she was part of everything bad that happened that day.

We had some deep conversations with six- and seven-year-olds.

Slowly, things got better. Teachers in my school were instrumental in building me up and coaching me to use different strategies. I went to the kids' soccer games and spent time at PTA meetings.

Through art and literacy, I was able to make personal connections. Their smiles and joy for learning brought a new kind of drive in me....how successful could we really all be? It was a busy year that brought me down and built me up. Many of these were the defining moments of why I chose to stay in this profession.

My career has been a roller coaster ride for eighteen years now.

There are some things that have gotten easier. While the perfect lesson plan doesn't exist, I can write one and know that it will be those teachable and unpredictable moments which make it stronger. I know many times I will bomb a lesson and when I do, I admit it. Nothing makes a class happier than knowing their teacher can actually make some big mistakes too. Note to self: They will never let you forget it.

In today's classrooms there is so much pressure to raise test scores. We collect and analyze data as if that had been our major in college.

Each day, we practice.

"Take your pencil out, write your name. Remember not to talk or peak at someone else's paper. I will repeat the question after I read it. Do your best." I probably sound like that teacher in the Charlie Brown specials.

We spend a lot of time giving these assessments.

All the other moments are made for why I continue to love teaching.

One year there was a little girl who loved to listen to me read. She was in my first-grade class and was struggling to keep up with our curriculum. When I read, her face would take on this faraway look as if she was dreaming of other things, yet she always asked questions about the book and wanted to hear more. Her personal life was hard too. A single mom was struggling to raise this little girl. One night after a long day at school, I finally got her mom on the phone. I had been trying to get in touch with her for weeks. Her mom explained a little about her own life. She used to have drug issues and there was never enough money, but she wanted so much more for her baby girl. This mom cried on the phone, and I promised her I would do everything I could to teach her baby. I did not have kids of my own at this time and so desperately wanted to do what I could to help. A few weeks later, my student was removed by social services and placed with her grandmother. Her heart was broken even though she loved her grandmother very much.

I continued to read and work at helping this little girl become successful. The court advocate came to speak with me about what was going on and there were so many needs. I know her mama wanted to do so much more for her, which is why I found myself shopping for new sneakers and new clothes for this girl who did not have much. I also got her some school supplies to keep at home so she could practice.

There was no college class to prepare me for this one either.

Her reading did improve. Slowly, her self-confidence began to build. She eventually left the school right after the year ended because of grandma living so far away. A couple of years later, I got a phone call from her and grandma. They were doing okay and missed me. I told them I hoped they stayed in touch. I never heard from them again.

It's been over ten years and I still wonder about her.

In teaching, one of the biggest lines we will tell you is that we want to make a difference. You will hear this echoed throughout the different professions within the education field.

Each year, there is a child. Any teacher can spot "the one." This child may have special needs. This can include a variety of things. Communication is a struggle or they need extra time to get their thoughts out. Hyperactivity can be enough to make a teacher dizzy. Sometimes there are social needs. It could be the child who comes to school angry with the chip on the shoulder. It might be the child who is hungry or struggles to learn what comes easily to others. Other students simply don't have very much at all. It is hard to go home at night knowing your classroom kids are hungry or do not have a mattress to sleep on. It's even harder to know that there is not a lot of love in their own homes.

That's the child I always want in my class.

This is the one who brings life into the classroom. It is also the one that needs structure, rules, and someone who cares. Throughout my career, I have learned that these are the stories that stay with me and give me the determination to show up each day.

At some point in a teaching career, we start to feel more confident. Classroom management has gotten stronger, our communication with parents gets better, and we have a tool box to help students progress in so many areas. However, just when we think it has gotten easier, something unexpected comes along.

This particular student arrived in the middle of the year. His parents dropped him off with worried faces. I reassured them that we would take good care of him. The special education teacher had been watching as well. She was going to be assisting me with him for forty-five minutes each day. He had special needs that we had to accommodate with resources that would help him be successful.

His hyperactivity did not allow for any quiet moments so it did not take him long to get comfortable. His parents had explained that the new medication would take some time to work. He had frequent outbursts throughout the day of calling out answers and interrupting his classmates and me. None of my go-to strategies were working. The special education teacher was trying her best as well. Due to some other issues, he also could not interpret all of the social cues his new friends were showing. He didn't understand personal space and he frequently became upset at recess with many of them. They also got upset. This created a very defeated dynamic for him.

I tried all sorts of ways to motivate him. We broke his day into small chunks of time and gave brain breaks in between subjects. I modeled the correct behavior and encouraged him to do the same. He didn't like to read because he could never focus long enough to use his strategies. Back and forth we went. When something would work, it would be short lived. It was so difficult to watch someone struggle so much when we knew he wanted to do so well.

One day, I made him the line leader. His face lit up as he started to tell everyone he had never had that job in a classroom before. Walking down the hall, he took his job very seriously. This kid who used to hop down the halls while singing or talking was walking calmly and quietly. Teachers walking the halls noticed and complimented him.

I gave him a pat on the shoulder. He looked up at me and said, "We found something I am good at, right, Mrs. Waltzer?"

Tears formed in my eyes. I gave him that job so I knew I could keep a better eye on him and he wouldn't bother his friends as much. The fact that it was turning out like this had nothing to do with my "why" of doing it. It was that moment that taught me to think of what these roles could do for a child who was struggling.

Looking back at him, I said, "There are so many more things we are going to find that you are good at. We won't give up."

And we didn't. The special education teacher and I worked harder than ever. Something had sparked in him. By the end of the year, he had friends and even read a book out loud to the class!

I will tell you though he still called out all the time. Sometimes we just can't work all the miracles.

One year I was teaching second grade. One of my favorite writing units to teach was poetry. I loved to show the kids how we could be creative using a variety of topics including people and places. A talented student chose to write a poem titled, "Love Is." She wrote it from the heart and it captured so many different feelings that kids and adults can relate to. I have kept this poem throughout the years and read it to all of my classes. It is so important for them to know that they are capable of love and also being loved. Academics are important but so are the things that make us good people. The people who can change the world for the better.

Teachers get to be a huge part of character education and we are proud.

I had stepped out of my classroom for a minute. When I walked back in, I took a moment to look around. Today was our first day and we were taking some time getting to explore the new areas in the room. A little boy was sitting in our classroom library. He had books spread all around him. While he looked at the pictures, he had pencils in his hand that were zooming around. It looked like he was playing airplane with them. He looked up at me and we made eye contact.

I smiled. There were some flashbacks going on through my mind. He reminded me of a child from another class. The years have a way of doing that.

This was going to be another memorable year.

STACEY WALTZER HIT HER FORTIES RUNNING COMPLETE WITH A TEACHING CAREER, HUSBAND, AND TWO LITTLE KIDS. NOT REALIZING THAT LIFE COULD GET EVEN MORE CRAZIER, SHE STARTED WRITING AND HASN'T STOPPED SINCE. WITH REAL-LIFE STORIES THAT READ LIKE FICTION, SHE EXISTS WITH THE HELP OF CAFFEINE AND LOTS OF LAUGHTER. SHE WAS ALSO PUBLISHED IN THE ANTHOLOGY, *THE UNOFFICIAL GUIDE TO SURVIVING PREGNANCY WITHOUT LOSING YOUR MIND* AND VARIOUS OTHER BLOGGING SITES. YOU CAN FIND HER AT 40WISHESAND-COUNTING.COM.

24

Small Awe
By Abigail Clark

y mother decided to become a teacher at forty, as mothers sometimes do. After all, we are the ones who choose our transitionary periods. From a consultant for federal education programs to the actual classroom. Three children and a master's in early childhood education. I don't really remember a time when my mom wasn't a teacher, self-absorbed as I was, but now she was integrated into the cycle of my day, in a way that felt as natural as rain.

Mom and I went to school together: her, for preschool; me, for second-grade. Every day before we left home, I'd fill a sippy cup of milk for the cereal she kept in her classroom. In the winter, I'd sit in the backseat on the way to school with a flannel blanket on my lap as she drummed her fingers to tinny pop music on the steering wheel. In the spring, it was still cold, but I'd feel the dew of the grass on my ankles as I waited, breath visible, the world barely awake. We were always quiet in the morning, watching as the world streaked past us. We strolled through the hallways the way we used to, when we were PTA mom and infant. All the walls were red bricks, and the carpets from the seventies, saturated as time, with unbreakable concrete just beneath the surface. The older teachers smiled as we passed. I grew within the same ecosystem, year after year, walls that changed gradually, with characters I recognized, and rituals I participated in without question. I loved it there. I still do.

The mornings would speed up. First I'd unstack the chairs, all a quarter of my height, then find the bean bag chair in the library and read until the first bell rang, signaling the time to take my leave. Steadily, the kids came in. I'd watch as Mom talked with the four-year-olds, and it was something you watch with small awe, a mastery rare and refined throughout the years. To connect with children, you must handle your universe with the wonder that they do; find a kind of majesty in dirt, paint, and rain. Then you must be respectful. I've noticed that people sometimes forget that children are people too, with thoughts and feelings and reactions that are all valid and valuable. You can talk to them like you know that. It's okay.

My mother was very good at the third thing you had to be.

You had to be giving. You had to understand circumstances. You needed to find your empathy within you and let it stream out. Mom taught vulnerable kids, hungry in more ways than one. All the time, poverty can steal people of their safety and security. Mom's seen children affected by lack of housing and medical care, racism, potential separation from their families. She understood the vastly different ways we grow.

Sometimes, when a child would have challenging behavior, they would become afraid of what mom would say to them after the heat of the moment. That primal fear within us, that somehow we are fundamentally unlovable, unforgivable.

Mom always told them they were a good person who made a mistake. She still loved them. She would always love them.

You can be flawed, spiteful, angry, but still good.

The four-year-olds in my mother's class sometimes told her they loved her. Before naptime, as she'd rub their backs. I forget how small that world is, how much bigger kindness becomes in that world.

Sometimes my brothers and I would correct her when she'd refer to her students as "her kids."

"My kids made soup out of the mud today!"

Or, "My kids are going to love this weaving project."

"We're your kids," we'd point out. "They're your students."

And she'd smile and nod, appeasing us a little, but I think somehow "her kids" meant all of us at the same time, an obvious secret we could never dream of knowing.

School comes with us wherever we go. My mother spends dollars and dollars at bookstores, thrift shops. She drives an hour to a shop for teachers, every month, for paper and markers the school can't afford. Museums, public parks, always a trip to the visitors center, always the question: "Are you open for field trips?"

When I was thirteen, my mother spoke to the manager at a restaurant. At every table, there was a pamphlet, declaring, "Vote NO on the meals tax!" And she spoke the way she always did to strangers, with a broad smile and emphatic gestures, asking why he wouldn't support legislation that would help fund schools. The man was at a loss of how to argue with someone so delightful.

They kept the pamphlets out. We haven't gone back since.

My mother carries the purse a student's mom gave her, constructed from traditional clothing made by the woman's aunt in Afghanistan, a family heirloom. She constantly worries about wearing it out.

I remember, when I'd finish odd jobs for her in the mornings, she'd always redo what I had done to some extent, in order to make it that much more right. I think it was how part of her nature manifested. My mom cared. I always admired that about her. Whatever she did, even if she made the wrong judgment in the moment, she always cared. About things people didn't notice, children that were overlooked or left behind. When no one else did.

I think that's part of why my mom decided to teach after years of consulting. Because of this deep capacity for care that exists within her, that looks the fear and the bleakness in the face and tells it no. Those feelings may not go away in a year or thirty, but at least they get told no every once in a while.

Every teacher has a little "save the world" within them. Sometimes it's a thankless job with Sundays filled with lesson plans and report cards, cuts in pay, and keen condescension from all sides. But those moments when Mom sees that stuffed animal she *knows* they would love, and her eyes light up in joy for her kids ... Because of the will to teach ... To bring some kind of joy and wonder to life ... To widen spaces of the world that may feel small ... *That's* teaching.

A couple of weeks ago, my mom and I went to visit my baby cousin, around three months old. A lot of the time he slept, but when he was awake, he wanted to look over my shoulder, survey what was happening under his watch. Until my mom took over. He loved watching her. She'd bounce him on her knee, and he wouldn't stop giggling and making nonsense noises, telling her how wonderful it was to have visitors. And as I watched my mom explain to him why he was smiling and babbling, years of child development spilling out, I couldn't help but think: It's remarkable how our hearts can emerge without prompting, without even trying.

ABIGAIL CLARK IS SEVENTEEN YEARS OLD AND HAS WRITTEN MANY WORDS. SHE ASPIRES TO WRITE MANY MORE. SHE LIKES TO DANCE, ESPECIALLY CONTEMPORARY AND MODERN. SHE ALSO PLAYS THE STRING BASS. WHEN SHE'S NOT ENGAGING IN THESE VARIOUS ACTIVITIES, SHE LOVES TO READ AND LEARN ABOUT DIFFERENT TYPES OF STORYTELLING. SHE LIVES IN VIRGINIA WITH HER FAMILY.

25

Jordan Rules
By Kerry Rossow

Her name was Mrs. Jordan and I adored her.

She was my fifth-grade teacher. She was almost six feet tall, wore pantsuits and huge jewelry. She drove a convertible, laughed loudly and there were rumors that she—*gasp*—drank beer. She was definitely not like our mothers or the other teachers in our small Indiana town.

I once overheard my mother say that Mrs. Jordan wore "city clothes." I never knew where one might buy city clothes. I just knew that she did *not* get her wardrobe at the Kmarts like the rest of us. (In Indiana, we like to put "the" in front of store names and they are always plural: *The* Kmarts or *The* Walmarts.)

Mrs. Jordan changed the trajectory of my life with one small sentence, "You should run for student council; people like you."

Shocking to those who know me now, I was painfully shy as a child. I would hide behind furniture if guests came a callin'. I am deaf in one ear and feared slurring my words or not being able to follow small talk so I said nothing. But I watched and listened to everything.

So, when Mrs. Jordan spoke those fateful words to little ole me, I was shocked. Had I heard her correctly? I didn't think anyone knew my name, much less *liked* me. I couldn't believe that she saw me that way. I was weird. Weird in the quiet five-foot-eleven fifth-grader, lurking about on the fringe kind of way. It never occurred to me that I was likeable and certainly not student council worthy. Student council girls were petite and bubbly and certainly did not carry both sides of imaginary conversations with themselves during their walks to school.

But Mrs. Jordan framed a version of me that I had never considered. Even if I had zero votes for student council, I vowed not to let down my idol. I braced for public humiliation but it would be worth it if I earned the approval of Mrs. Jordan.

Miracle of all miracles, I ran and was elected to Liberty Middle School student council. I spent the next seven years on student council. I pushed myself to speak to others—not just imaginary in-the-shower conversations—and I spoke loud enough for others to actually hear me!

I'm still weird, still five-eleven, and still deaf in one ear. I'm the most outgoing shy person you will ever meet. Before any social event, I sit in my swagger wagon, giving myself a Mrs. Jordan pep talk. I change all the "what if" thoughts into "even if" thoughts.

"*What if* there is a lot of background noise, I slur my words, and people think I'm drunker than a monkey?"

"*Even if* people think I'm drunker than a monkey, at least I'll have an excuse to leave early."

See how that works?

Student council was like a gateway drug but in a good way. Wait...I'm not saying that gateway drugs are good. Gateway drugs are definitely bad. (See? Still awkward!) I am trying to say that student council was a bridge to other opportunities—from sororities to PTA to public speaking.

Life has a way of coming full circle. I am now a teacher. I know the power of my words. I know the power of acknowledgment. I know the power of seeing and being seen. I know that one small comment from a teacher in a small Indiana town to a weird fifth-grade girl standing slouched over, hip cocked to appear shorter, was a huge, life-changing gift.

Here I am, almost forty years later. I'm almost six feet tall, I laugh loudly, I like my beer, I wear pantsuits and huge jewelry, and I channel Mrs. Jordan every single day when my students walk through the door.

KERRY ROSSOW LEFT TEACHING AFTER EIGHTEEN YEARS IN THE CLASSROOM AND FOUND HER WRITING VOICE ON HER BLOG, HOUSE-TALKN, AND IS THE PROUD CO-FOUNDER OF THE SHE SAID PROJECT. SHARING HER LIFE SHENANIGANS, KERRY BECAME A WEEKLY COLUMNIST AT IN THE POWDER ROOM. IN 2013, FOLLOWING THE MOTTO "LEAP AND THE NET WILL APPEAR," KERRY TOOK HER FIRST MISSION TRIP TO HAITI, BECAME A PUBLISHED AUTHOR IN THE BESTSELLING ANTHOLOGY, *I JUST WANT TO PEE ALONE*, AND *YOU HAVE LIPSTICK ON YOUR TEETH*, AND TOOK TO THE STAGE AS PART OF THE CASTS IN LISTEN TO YOUR MOTHER 2013 AND 2014. HER WRITING HAS BEEN FEATURED ON *THE HUFFINGTON POST*, SCARY MOMMY, AND RANTS FROM MOMMYLAND. SHE HAS COME FULL CIRCLE AND RETURNED TO THE MONTESSORI SCHOOL OF CU —BECAUSE SIX-YEAR-OLDS LAUGH AT ALL OF HER DUMB JOKES!

26

Lost and Found
By Holly Rutchik

Personally, I was never a huge fan of school. Intelligent enough, I fared well in college, where you can focus on your area of interest. Before that, though, school was a different story. My high school principal threatened me with truancy court because I refused to attend science class each day, asserting that a ringing bell telling me I HAD to study physics each day from 9 a.m. to 9:52 a.m. was insane. To this day, I hold strong to that life theory.

Here is the burn of adulthood: I have a husband, five children, numerous family medical conditions, and a full-time corporate job. And yet, school is my number one stress. Our kids have to go. I can't *not* send them just because their mother doesn't dig schedules. Mad props to the homeschoolers; I would literally spoon my eyes out if I was in charge of a curriculum (or a schedule for that matter). In our house, daily clean underwear and proper checks of the school folders are struggle enough.

When you add to that mix a difficult child (one who doesn't learn traditionally) you need to set the bar low for yourself to survive. Who cares about grades? If they don't get kicked out, it's a good day.

Being the parent of a student you know is going to be the kid who drives the teacher to drink at night is a stress only a parent who has gotten "that" call from school can understand.

Most parents hope their kids fare well socially at school. In the early years you hope they don't eat their boogers or piss themselves in front of their peers for fear of them be labeled a freak or worse yet, ignored altogether.

That being said, a mom's worries for her unique kiddo don't really rest on the shoulders of ten-year-olds on a playground. Nope, those "crotch goblins" (as I once overheard a teacher refer to the kids in her class) aren't the concern. The key to the school year is the teacher.

Don't believe me? Ask any parent who has obsessively checked their emails to find out which teacher their kid got assigned to. With each new school year, I await teacher announcements like a contestant on *The Bachelor*. Will my kid get the rose—and be liked by the teacher? As on *The Bachelor*, the traditionally "all-American" girls need not worry. The sweet sunshine of polite little girls batting their eyelashes goes a long way. I know: I have some of those in my home too. (I have a million kids.)

But then there's my special little gal. The one who sits in the back of the glass drawing horses. Sometimes, when she's in a mood, she spends entire days communicating only in animals noises. Every class has one. And she's mine. My gal—with her ADHD, her slightly alarming concern for animals over people and her flapping arms—doesn't even have eyelashes.

Our daughter has trichotillomania, an impulse control disorder that creates an urge to pull out one's body hair. She picks out her eyelashes, and the rest is a surprise. Sometimes, she discards them on the kitchen floor or glues them to a piece of paper. When she runs out of eyelashes, she resorts to picking them off the sleeping eyelids of her little sisters in the middle of the night. She's a go-getter, my little monster.

This summer, she had no eyelashes or eyebrows. As the school year approached, my anxiety grew. Would the teacher find my kid's habits of picking her hair out (while not doing a damn thing she's told) endearing or annoying as fuck? I am the mother of what boils down to an exposed nerve of a person.

An exposed nerve can emote and create like a genius. But an exposed nerve can also hurt like a mofo.

Our kids all attend a private, faith-based school. That school has gone above and beyond to accommodate our alternatively brilliant gal. There have been meetings, special aides assigned to help with tracking homework, numerous fidgets toys purchased out of the personal pockets of overly-dedicated and underpaid teachers and even homemade weighted lap pillows—all in the name of helping our daughter.

Not once has her different learning style been viewed as a negative. Every meeting has started with naming our daughter's strengths, and a reminder to keep them at the forefront of the conversation as we discuss how to work together to assist her.

In our school, though, fourth grade is the big leagues. There is real work to be done, intense work about which this mother with a master's degree hasn't a clue. I knew it would be a rough year. And I was right.

For starters, the academics were a challenge. On a geography test, my girl labeled the waterways of Wisconsin as her favorite snack items. The Mississippi River was labeled as "snickerdoodles." And Lake Michigan? "Cheeseburgers." The map looked delicious, but it struck me with the fear of God harder than an unexpected medical bill.

"Damn it, child!" I yelled as my husband handed me the test. "You realize that if you piss off these teachers, you're screwed, right?! Your 'you-ness' is almost lost on these people!"

The look my husband gave me told me that I might have fallen off the tightrope of acceptable parenting. Later, after our geography whiz had gone to bed, my husband and I discussed our options.

"I'm so disappointed," he said. "We studied for that test. She knows those rivers."

"Who cares about the test or the grade?!" I yelled. "Her teachers are going to hate her! They're complaining about how disrespectful this is, and they're giving her a zero! If they hate her, it's over."

Another test came home with "Very Disappointed" scrawled across the top. Apparently, she had been given the chance to improve her twenty-some percent on the test and had declined outright. My annoyance now shifted to the teacher. No more do-overs? "Disappointed?" Does this lady not get it? Our daughter is literally pulling her hair out!

Around the same time, the trichotillomania started to spread. After nearly two years of focusing on her eyebrows and lashes, our daughter started to pull hair from the top of her head. Within two weeks, she was rocking the worst kind of mullet I've ever seen. (And I was raised in a small town best known for the grand national truck and tractor pull.)

We started getting more emails from school. Mama became angry.

"She's not paying attention."

"She gets angry at people."

"She's stealing."

Make a list of the calls about schoolwork and behavior a parent doesn't want to get and I've gotten that call.

We took each situation and tried our best to be A+ parents of a problem student, hoping the grade would average out and she wouldn't be expelled.

We get it: she's different! She's brilliant but not in the way that works for school. She's a handful. My fear bread anger and this mama started to set my ranging eyes on the school as my child started to pick out more and more hair.

And then a new email came in from the school:

"I am concerned that, after she pulls the stands of hair out, she either sucks on the pieces of hair or possibly eats them," the teacher wrote.

"I get it, lady! You're disappointed and our kid is a freak," I snapped back to no one as I read her words.

"I'm obviously not a doctor," the email continued.

"No, you're not. Take two steps to the left and back the hell on off," I replied (again, to the air).

"...it could be very dangerous to her health," the email concluded.

"So, we're bad parents," my husband grumbled as he poured fuel on my fire.

The school wanted to speak to the entire class about the hair-pulling, and explain what trichotillomania is to the children as they were noticing the pulling. The psychologist advised we not do this unless our daughter agreed, and she continued to refuse.

"Everyone thinks I'm weird, mama," she confided in me. "I don't want them to know, because I'm hoping someday I'll make a friend. I want to know what it feels like to have a friend."

"We don't have to tell anyone anything," I choked out. "I promise."

"I promise" is pretty much the worst thing you can accidentally say to a child. But after hearing that, I would have let her juggle knives or get a face tattoo.

The school pushed again, pointing out that our daughter was noticeably bald and that kids talk. They insisted that giving ten-year-old kids the information would only help, not hinder.

I sat my kid down and lied through my teeth when I told her I was sure this was the best thing to do and that Daddy and I one hundred percent trusted her teacher and principal to teach her class about hair-pulling without making her seem like a freak.

The next day, the principal and teacher discussed our daughter with her peers while I stress-ate Doritos for lunch. Within twenty-four hours, the messages from other parents started pouring in:

One parent wrote, "Our daughter told us about the meeting at school today, and how your daughter's brain was made different in lots of cool ways. She's so brave."

"I was moved to tears when our daughter told us about the meeting at school today," wrote another. "It was true community how the principal tied the message of love and acceptance in to sharing your daughter's struggle and gave the kids ideas on how they could help their friend."

The following week was the year's best at school, socially and academically. She was allowed to go outside of dress code and wear hats or bandannas, and her peers made an extra effort to make her feel good about herself.

"I made a friend at recess," was the report the next Friday. "And Ms. S. gave me this."

From her backpack, she removed a thick hairband that was purple (her favorite color) with horses (her favorite animal). It was clearly purchased with intention as a gift to a struggling student from a teacher who truly cares.

Her classmates started asking her about swimming (she's a star swimmer) and her interest in animals—aspects of her personality unrelated to trichotillomania or her academic performance.

She also developed another hidden talent: singing. We've known for some time she is a gifted vocalist, but she has always been too nervous to sing in front of people, eventually becoming physically ill and backing out.

We were shocked to hear from our oldest child that our special ten-year-old had auditioned for a solo in the school Christmas concert. "She sang in front of all those students to audition?" I asked.

It was true. Later that day, the music teacher informed us that she wanted to give our girl the solo. However, she wanted check with us first. Reluctantly, we agreed. We knew our daughter had the pipes for it, but we wondered whether her stage fright would overtake her, forcing her to back out, and embarrass herself.

On the day of the dress rehearsal, she went to the school office, complaining that she was sick and asking to come home. When I saw the school's number (and then a voicemail) pop up on my phone, I promptly ducked out of my work meeting.

The principal had called to say that our girl was sick, but she was also too nervous to sing. He wondered if, maybe (with her other struggles) it would be best to reassign the solo.

I had to get back to my meeting, and I couldn't call him back. I desperately wanted, when I got home from work, to convince our girl to do her solo.

That afternoon, I picked her up from school, and she could barely walk. She became ill the second she walked through the door. I pulled our older daughter aside. "Did they reassign the solo?" I asked.

"No," our eldest replied. "I tried to hug her and tell her she didn't have to do it. But Ms. S told me to go away and leave her be."

"WHAT?!" I yelled. "You are her sister. What is the matter with this teacher?"

"No, Mom," our eldest clarified. "Ms. S told me to not talk about her being sick. Ms. S said she needs to know she can do it."

Ms. S didn't let our girl slink off, and our girl crushed that solo. After the concert, members of our school community rallied around her with praise.

Yes, school is the hardest part of our life right now. Every day, there are social, academic and impulse control struggles, and every night, there are three-plus hours of homework. However, we know our school community is behind us, celebrating our daughter as she learns to celebrate her strengths while taking on her challenges, including trichotillomania. The teachers, staff and community of our school are all helping her find herself as she loses her hair.

HOLLY RUTCHIK, M.A., (Minivan Matriarch) is an inspirational writer and speaker. She believes in using words for encouragement. The floor of her minivan is littered with books, magazines, journals, and coloring pages, only some of which belong to her five young children. She lives in Wisconsin with Mr. Minivan Matriarch and her million kids. Hollyrutchik.com.

27

A Letter of Recognition
By Candy Mickels Mejia

The letter in my hand was addressed to me specifically. The return address belonged to my English teacher, Ms. Jane. Being a teenager, I wasn't used to getting any mail at all so to get a letter from a teacher, especially while I was in the hospital, was inconceivable.

I didn't have a close relationship with any of my teachers. I was a good student and felt like they liked me well enough, but I was also an avid rule follower and it felt very against the rules to get to know a teacher personally. To me the teachers didn't seem like regular adults or parents; they were The Authority Figures around whom I must tiptoe with prudence.

Maybe if I'd known my teachers for many years as my classmates had I would have felt differently, but this was only my second year at our small-town school. As a freshman in high school I couldn't compete with friends who had been in the community since grade school or before. It felt kind of like joining a family by marriage, which was the reason I had to move to this small town in the first place.

It wasn't clear to me then if the specifics of my diagnosis had been shared with my teachers and classmates, so I couldn't imagine what Ms. Jane would've sent me. It definitely looked like a letter; it was too small to be a card. It was sealed, so I knew my mom hadn't read it yet. I waited to open it, though, since my nerves felt too delicate to read whatever my favorite teacher had sent. I decided to first open the small stack of Get Well cards that had been part of the delivery.

Among the cards was one from my teammates on the junior girls basketball team, one from my always chatty keyboarding class, one from a group of people who had become my friends over the previous year and a half, and one from my little sister's fifth-grade class. My well-wishers were now all two hours away from me as I recovered from surgery in my hospital bed, so it was a nice little wave from the town that had become home to me and from the school community that was its foundation.

That was not the last stack of cards I would receive over the next few months. Though my chemotherapy would be planned, I didn't know then I'd have two more surgeries in my near future, one of which would have me in the hospital during Valentine's Day. I also didn't know the amount of prayer lists I'd be on or that the community would organize a spaghetti supper to raise money to help my family during that time.

My mom and stepdad had only been married a couple of years at that point. He was disabled and my mom had three jobs and no medical insurance. This was not a terribly unusual situation in the rural community where we lived and where my stepdad had grown up. But it was not a situation we wanted to be in when I was diagnosed with cancer at fifteen.

The hospital stay that followed the major abdominal surgery to remove a football-sized tumor from my body is the first time I remember being in a hospital. It was easy to forget that the world was carrying on outside while I practiced walking upright and taking prescribed deep breaths to prevent pneumonia. After reading through the cards I was reminded of what the rest of my world was doing, and that they were well and normal and that they did not have cancer.

Get Well Soon is a thoughtful message, but it's also shorthand for "I don't really understand what's going on with you, but I wish that it wasn't"—nice enough, but also a reminder of the isolation that is created by extreme or unusual circumstances. It was comforting to know my friends and classmates and teachers were thinking of me, but it also emphasized how I was once again an outsider, like I'd been when I was the new girl the previous school year.

Ms. Jane's letter was the only envelope that remained sealed. I fiddled with the envelope and tore across the top edge to find a perfectly folded piece of paper inside. As I unfolded the letter, I saw Ms. Jane's perfect handwriting perfectly lined up in sentences that filled the unlined paper.

Ms. Jane could be stern but was always kind. She wore red lipstick and red nail polish and had the best laugh, but she could also stop you in your tracks with just a look, especially if you crumpled a piece of paper in her classroom. At the first sound of a crumple, Ms. Jane would raise her head from her desk and shoot her gaze around the room, trying to pinpoint the culprit. The look in her eyes was enough to stop you from whatever you were doing, and enough to make you second guess ever handling paper again.

She loved diagramming sentences. Prior to my eighth-grade English class, I didn't even know what that was. I'll admit, though, that even today I often mentally break down sentences in diagrams when I am constructing them. Ms. Jane also introduced us to *To Kill a Mockingbird* in eighth grade. To bring that story into the consciousness of a class full of young teens in rural Arkansas was like a superpower; the experience changed me for good.

So here I was, reading a letter from this force of a woman, and it was more personal than I expected. I skimmed the letter first, too nervous to settle in on one sentence. I then took a breath (as deeply as my newly incised abdomen would allow) and reread it at a digestible pace.

Ms. Jane shared with me that years before, she too had been diagnosed with cancer. She wrote that she was "so sorry" I was going through this but that she understood some of the thoughts and feelings I was having and that my attitude would be critically important to my recovery.

I had just turned fifteen the week before, so I wasn't yet (nor am I now) a master of my emotions, but her words connected with me on a level I hadn't expected. I felt seen in a way I didn't know I needed to be seen.

She went on to write, "Be positive. Be determined. Grit your teeth. Let nothing stand in the way of your recovery."

Reading that letter in 1990, I did not have a view of the greater world to which to apply that perspective, nor did I have visions of my future. I only had what was right in front of me: I was sick and I needed to heal.

Ms. Jane knew that. She didn't try to make that chapter in my life something it wasn't. There was no "things happen for a reason" banter or "you will be stronger because of this" promise. She was writing with the frankness of a survivor. She recognized the struggle I was facing by sharing the struggle she herself had faced.

I refolded the letter on its already perfect lines and put it back in its envelope. It lived with the other cards and notes I received and made its way back home with me.

When I returned to school after that first hospital stay, I still had restrictions on what I could lift and what I could do since I was recovering from major surgery. My friends took turns carrying my purse and my books and escorted me down our one hall to make sure no one ran into me. They took care of me. Even if it was in part because of the novelty of the idea of being my bodyguards, it still felt every bit like the support it was meant to be.

Each teacher acknowledged my absence and my return as they welcomed me back to class. I could feel every set of eyes in the room on me, and could feel my face flush while I held my breath waiting for the teacher to finally segue into class work.

Ms. Jane greeted me with a smile, which I returned, though I felt more self-conscious in her class now that I knew I was on her radar. I did not want her to think her words were wasted on me. I also did not know how to thank her for her letter -- the thought of doing so summoned a knot in my stomach and panic in my head.

Two weeks later when I was terribly sick from chemotherapy, the words from her letter scrolled through my brain: *Be determined. Grit your teeth.* I did my best, trying to stick it out for a week of making the two hour drive to and from the hospital every day with my IV hanging from my arm, not sure whether I was feeling like I was about to fall asleep or about to vomit. Another week later her words stuck with me when I had an emergency complication from the prior surgery and had to have another surgery to correct it: *Your attitude right now is critically important. Be positive.*

By the time I returned to school again I'd lost twenty pounds and most of my hair. All eyes were on me once again, but my appearance wasn't the only reason.

The school had put up a "Welcome Back" banner for me at the end of our one hallway, along with a painting created by an amazing artist at our school. Everyone, and I mean quite possibly each and every person, had signed the banner welcoming me back to school.

I looked like a shell of myself hidden under a hat and a little makeup. Again each of my teachers acknowledged my return but each was also accommodating, making sure I would let them know if I needed anything, though besides a nap I can't imagine what I would have needed at that point.

When I first saw Ms. Jane after my second return to school, we exchanged knowing looks. I had changed since my previous homecoming; chemotherapy and its side effects had been brutal and I wasn't done yet. While others looked at me with pity and wonder, Ms. Jane knew that even though I looked like a (still smiling) shell of myself, I was gritting my teeth and doing the work I needed to do to recover.

LAST SUMMER while I was scrolling through Facebook, I stopped at a post from Ms. Jane's daughter, with whom I'd reconnected in our adult years. Ms. Jane had died.

I sat with the news for a few minutes, taking a deep breath as if that would help me accept the loss. I thought again about the letter she wrote me and how much I appreciated her sharing that bit of herself with me. I'm not sure I ever thanked her for that, but I hope she knew to some degree how her words stuck with me.

My youngest child had her own medical emergency during her last break from school: her appendix ruptured. She's a tough kid, but after we'd been in the ER for a while she started to get worn down.

As her mom, I felt fear start to creep in. I wanted to help her feel less alone but I didn't know how to comfort her. She was tired, weak, and a little afraid. Looking at my eight-year-old lying in that hospital bed reminded me of when I was the child in the hospital. I held her hand and knelt down closer to her as I recalled a message that had comforted me once.

"I'm so sorry this is happening to you," I told her, "but stay positive. Your good attitude will help you recover faster and get home more quickly. I never liked being in the hospital either, but I'm OK now, and you will be too."

She squeezed my hand, pressed her lips together, and nodded her head. I kissed her on her forehead and closed my eyes, inhaling the sticky, sweet scent of my baby girl.

I hope to some degree those words, or at least their intent, stay with my daughter the way Ms. Jane's letter stayed with me.

CANDY MICKELS MEJIA IS A WRITER AND MOM WHO LIVES JUST OUTSIDE OF HOUSTON. SHE WRITES ABOUT PARENTING, MIDLIFE, AND MENTAL HEALTH. YOU CAN READ MORE OF HER WORK ON HER BLOG, SLIGHTLY OVERCAFFEINATED, OR FIND HER ON TWITTER_@CMICKELSMEJIA.

28

The Multiple Talents of First Grade's Mrs. Friedrich
By Beth Markley

"One two three, eyes on me," Mrs. Friedrich said in a clear voice, her hand raised, palm out, imposing as a Sherman tank at the front of the classroom. All of five foot, two inches of don't-you-dare-mess-with-me.

"One. Two. Eyes on you," twenty first-graders responded in unison, turning to face the front of the room. Their chatter died to nothing.

It was moments like these I'd remember for years afterward: a petite woman with steely nerves stilling every one of nearly two-dozen wriggling bodies and their wagging tongues with a word. Before I'd known it was possible, I'd have chosen flight as my super-power, or maybe settled for the ability to read a book in a moving vehicle without getting queasy.

Now I wanted this.

"We're going to tone things down or move on to something else," she said. "I can't even hear myself *think* in this room." She made eye contact with one student, then another, and then a third, her lips pursed. No one moved, terrified of whatever that "something else" might be. A word puzzle? A spelling worksheet? Dear God, *math*?

After letting them ponder the what-ifs for a full minute, Mrs. Friedrich returned to the pile of papers at her desk. Everyone in the room exhaled at once, and then picked up their respective crayons or glue sticks or blunt-tipped scissors to return to work.

Activity resumed, this time at a low hum, and I stifled the urge to applaud.

Our son's first-grade teacher didn't fit either the "fresh young thing" mold, nor that of "wizened mentor." She was in her mid-thirties, with the reserved air of some of her more tenured colleagues, and the manner of an old-fashioned schoolmarm.

I asked Jack (now a college freshman) what he remembered about her.

"She used to say she wished she had a taser to keep us all in line," he said, which tracks with the impression I recall.

Jack was new to the school that fall, having attended a Montessori program through kindergarten. The year had barely begun when rumors of Mrs. Friedrich's sternness reached me, as well as news that a number of the previous year's kindergartener moms had collectively decided they wanted their children placed with one of the other first-grade teachers.

This would be (coincidentally or not, I'm not sure), the last year parents could request specific teachers in advance, the last year the involved parents could collectively pre-assess the classrooms into which their little darlings would matriculate.

Those who did so were the PTA parents, the folks who volunteered for field trips and art projects. They were the bringers of snacks for holiday parties, the collectors of money for class fundraisers. They were parents who knew their children's teachers' names because they called them regularly to discuss homework assignments or floundering grades. They were the parents who wouldn't dream of letting a month's worth of handouts languish in their child's backpack or forget to leave an encouraging note in a sack lunch.

These were the people I met at the first day social hour on the playground, handing out muffins and pouring coffee. They were the ones I expected to get to know a little better the night of the parent orientation. Instead, they all filed into the other rooms of the teachers they'd pre-selected last spring, while Jack's dad and I left them for Mrs. Friedrich's class, where we made up about a third of the crowd —a small squad tucking our knees under desks crafted for munchkins.

Mrs. Friedrich's volunteer sign-up sheet made its way around our small group with lightning speed. I signed up as a reading buddy. I looked at Mike for a second before signing him up as well. At the end of the session I returned to the sheet and nabbed slots for organizing holiday parties and to lead an art project or two.

Our names did precious little to fill up the still nearly blank page, so I took the liberty of signing my parents up to join us.

I was *pretty* sure it would be okay with them. Jack was their first grandchild, for whom they'd have moved mountains, and I had a solid memory of Mom volunteering for a few elementary school activities, and as my first Girl Scout troop leader, despite being among the minority of full-time working moms. For her, this grade school gig would be familiar territory.

Dad was a different story. He'd been so infrequently involved in my grade school years that the one and only afternoon he'd taken off work to pick me up after the last bell, my best friend told the playground duty she'd seen me leaving in a stranger's car. We arrived home from skating lessons to find cops parked in our driveway.

By the time Jack came along—Dad's namesake—he was considerably less busy at work and quite a bit more interested in the childrearing process. I was early into my freelance career and took advantage, recruiting him to babysit when I needed time for meetings.

Having hailed from an era where fathers didn't change diapers, fix snacks, or have any idea where we kept the peanut butter, Dad took to the care of his grandson with the fervor of an ex-con who'd found

Jesus. Jack was the only member of our family invited to squeeze next to him in his recliner and grab chubby handfuls of cheese puffs from the bag that had always been off limits to my sister and me.

When Dad became Mrs. Friedrich's designated Tuesday reading buddy, he realized how much he had to learn about the life and times of an average six-year-old. He threw himself into the task.

As autumn passed, we compared notes about our respective classroom experiences.

"Did you see Jacob's new crew cut?" I said, "he announced to the whole class he had lice."

"Noah speaks so low I can hardly hear him," Dad said. He had a hard time hearing almost everyone, so this was no surprise. "And Sally needs glasses. She holds the book right up to her nose."

"I know," I said. Sally *had* glasses, actually, ones she often removed at her father's house and then forgot when her mom picked her up. It was a problem Sally and I had discussed with some frequency. Mrs. Friedrich possessed a drawer full of spares and extras: mittens for kids who forgot theirs, trail mix and granola bars for those who'd slept through breakfast. But she didn't have a spare set of glasses for Sally.

"That Ian's a smart kid," Dad told me. "Does Jack play with Ian at recess?"

"No, Jack plays with Nate sometimes, though."

"Oh," he said. We were both familiar with Nate.

"Nate, buddy, don't you have a clean shirt at home?" Mrs. Friedrich asked one morning while we were getting into a book. It did look like he'd left a good sampling of his breakfast on his chest.

"Nope. Mom said if I won't pick up the damn clothes off the floor, she's not going to bother with my laundry," he said. He planted his hands on his hips and tilted his chin in what I took to be his best mom imitation. His precociousness made me smile, and I turned my head so he wouldn't see. I remembered Mrs. Friedrich warning us at orientation she'd be privy to a good portion of our home lives and wouldn't judge. Neither would I.

Nate's mom, having missed orientation, was probably unaware of Nate's imitations of her, expletives and all.

"I see," Mrs. Friedrich said, not commenting on the language. "Back to work then."

I did have the opportunity to make the acquaintance of Nate's mom one afternoon. Jack and I were leaving school early for an appointment as Nate was showing her in through the school foyer. She was holding the hand of an unwilling toddler, the other arm hooked through the handle of an infant seat. Her exhaustion contrasted Nate's exuberance.

"Hey Jack, you *gotta* see my new baby!" he said, grabbing my son's hand. The boys peered into the carrier. Nate's mom waited, looking ready to drop. I smiled at her but couldn't catch her eye. The toddler squirmed in her grasp.

Later that week, at the class holiday party, Nate and I were decorating mice ornaments cut from felt, trying to hold the fabric straight while he drew on whiskers with black marker. Both of us were getting more ink on our hands than the mouse was getting whiskers.

"Mom told me there isn't a Santa," he said.

"Is that so?" I said, in a low voice, looking around the room to see if anyone was listening.

"Yep. But then the neighbors brought a bunch of big boxes for Christmas and a whole *damn* tree just for us!" He stopped to grab my arm with markered hands. "Now she *has* to admit he's real!"

"Inside voice, please, Nate," Mrs. Friedrich said, a little more gently than I would have expected. She was working with Sally, who'd remembered her glasses that day and was pouring mounds of silver glitter on the cutout of a stocking. Nate's face glowed, I wiped a cookie crumb off his chin, resisting the urge to pull him into a hug.

"Awesome, Nate! That makes me so happy!" I said.

Christmas passed for us that year in its traditional whirlwind of decorations and visitors and guests and food. I couldn't stop thinking about Nate. I wondered about the supplies brought by his neighbors, envisioning his mom pulling food and presents from boxes, one by one, exclaiming over every container of stuffing mix and packet of saltines.

Or would she be subdued and melancholy? Resentful of her situation, worried about how she'd continue to provide after the holiday? Was she still as overwhelmed and tired as the day I'd seen her in the foyer?

I was looking forward to catching up with Nate after the break, but when school resumed and I returned to Mrs. Friedrich's classroom, his desk was empty.

"They're homeschooling now," Mrs. Friedrich told me. "Mom had a hard time getting him in by the bell, and I guess she was tired of being reprimanded." I nodded. Latecomers to campus were escorted from the playground directly to the office where I imagined they heard principal Bowdan recite his mantra that headed every parent newsletter and email and capped off the voicemail message on the school phone: "Miss a minute, miss a *lot*."

After a month, Nate returned to class for another try. We greeted each other with glee, then got down to business gluing valentine hearts on a shoebox, leaving space to cut a hole in the top. He was characteristically boisterous. Mrs. Friedrich reminded him twice to use his inside voice, then let the matter slide.

Nate was gone again the following week.

He'd been pulled from class for the rest of the year, Mrs. Friedrich told me, after the baby he'd introduced to Jack that sunny afternoon failed to wake from his nap one morning and Nate's mom's resolve to drop her oldest son off in advance of the bell evaporated.

"One less rascal to worry about," she said, not looking at me but at his empty desk in the front row. She folded her arms in front of her, a corner of her lips turned down.

Right then, in a room full of kids, all quietly working as they'd been instructed to do, I had an insight so clear it made my eyes sting. For some of these children, especially the ones who could use a few more engaged adults in their lives, Mrs. Friedrich had to be the unfailing one, the one who held them accountable for their reading goals, who noticed when they didn't dress warmly enough or couldn't concentrate because they were hungry; this ragtag group of six-year-olds with breakfast on their shirts and chronically misplaced glasses. She had to be reliable. Solid. Theirs. She propped them all up with sternness, buoyed by her snarky sense of humor. She kept them all afloat.

Until she had no other choice but to let go.

Here I was, meandering in and out of her classroom, presenting myself as what I hoped was a model of stability in the lives of kids like Nate. But I, with my scant once or twice weekly visits, was wrecked at this news. Just this one kid. I didn't think I could bear it over and over every year.

Mrs. Friedrich, on the other hand, returned. Resolute, unfailing as she had to be, for Nate and all of the rest of them, as long as she had them.

Forget silencing a room of first graders, *that* was her superpower.

Mrs. Friedrich had moved to the fifth grade by the time our younger son started school, and then on to another school not much later. Subsequent teachers had filled their volunteer rosters by the time we got to the parent meeting. We never had the opportunity to volunteer *en masse* as a family again but satisfied ourselves with the occasional chaperoning gig for field trips and school dances.

We had the opportunity to get to know all types of instructors in the years after that, from the effusively bubbly to the chronically crabby, and everything in between. I came to realize Mrs. Friedrich's drawer full of mittens and stocking caps and granola bars was similar to those many teachers kept stocked for their students.

I wondered if each of these teachers also had their own superpowers to bring to bear for the Sallys who forgot their glasses and the Nates with their outdoor voices and all the other children who wandered into and out of their lives. I wondered, as well, if they had coping mechanisms for when those powers were no longer needed.

I couldn't always see them, but from that year on, I always looked.

BETH MARKLEY LIVES IN IDAHO WITH HER HUSBAND, TWO ALMOST

GROWN SONS, AND A RECLUSIVE BROWN DOG. SHE BLOGS ABOUT PARENTING MISHAPS, TRAVEL, RUNNING, AND IN LIFE IN GENERAL AT MIDLIFE SENTENCE. SHE HAS BEEN FEATURED ON *THE HUFFINGTON POST*, MAMALODE, WHAT THE FLICKA, SCARY MOMMY, AND ERMA BOMBECK'S WRITER'S WORKSHOP.

29

The Class Before PE
By Mackenzie Plieskatt

We are instructed to write in our notebooks, to fully dissolve into a person who was there in the trenches. The one thing I particularly like about my history teacher, Mr. Southworth, is how in depth he is in everything he does. This is perhaps my favorite simulation, as he added a writing aspect to it.

It's 1914 and I'm currently in the middle of the trenches in Northern France. I think soldiers were terrified of many things, not any one thing in particular. They feared what most people would if they were in a situation like this: death. Not knowing if one gunshot was going to be followed by more. They had many other things on their mind in between gunshots, they feared if a simple injury would be the death of them, or if they'd run out of food and water. They thought of not being able to come home at all, and not ever seeing their family again. But whatever the fears, they culminated into a traumatic experience for all, or at least a traumatic experience for me. I could not understand how anyone would not be afraid in a situation like this. I was afraid, and I was their medic, it was my job to eliminate their fear asthey battled both death and the bullets flying over our head.

A loud *thunk* brings me from 1914 to 2018, and I suddenly recall we are in a classroom where the sounds are blocks hitting the wooden tables we are crouched underneath, and the tickling feeling is not fear or bullets, but dusters on our backs. We're in the middle of our Trench Warfare unit and Mr. Southworth has gone all out on this simulation. After every couple of units, he does one, so we can feel what many did in the time period we're studying. He instructs us to put our pencils down, as it was time for another round of the dusters and banging on the table.

The world is in chaos; bombshells litter the ground and I can't see a single sign of hope amidst the cloudy skies and panicked screams. We're here to fight to the end, but I'm not sure I can handle it anymore. Maintaining mental and physical stability through all of this is nearly impossible, despite all of our training. I don't know how anyone could prepare for something like this. Each shot begins a new, separate war. Not just with the enemy, but within ourselves. Constant thoughts rush through our heads, wondering if we're next, and if we'll even live to see another day. Wondering if well ever be able to caress our kid's cheeks, or if we'll ever be able to tell them "It'll be okay" again. Wondering if our whole life is going to be wiped away clean, because of one single bullet. Another medic next to me squeals in fright, and I look over at the body he was handed. The man he holds has grey hair, caked with mud and blood and his eyes are a piercing emerald color. I don't see anything wrong with him as I let my eyes skim over his body. But, as I reach his legs, I too am horrified by the sight. He's missing everything from the knee cap below, and I realize that there's no saving him. This was too much for a few medics.

Mr. Southworth is reading from a book now, but his words sound so jumbled I can barely make them out. All I can focus on is how this simulation feels as if we really were sitting in a trench right now, and the story that continues to play out in my mind. He projects a few images up onto the screen and we all are given a glimpse of what people really did look like during this time. In those flashes of picture on the screen, we see real faces; soldiers sitting in trenches, medics gathered around.

The mask we're assigned to wear for gas attacks makes me feel claustrophobic and sick. Letting out a breath of warm air, my vision suddenly becomes very cloudy. Panic runs through me, what if an enemy comes and I can't see them? I'd be letting down our troop- not only them, but our whole side of the war. I want to make an effort to pull my mask up, only a little. Just to make my foggy vision go away. But it was no use, it was not worth it to risk my life. I have a daughter and wife I need to return to. If I lift up my mask just for clear vision, my life would end. I could definitely deal with this over death.

He waits for us to stop writing, then proceeds to read aloud from the book again. I begin to pull at my own mask (really just the thing nurses use), feeling claustrophobic and sick myself. I want to lift it up, just a little bit, but then I remember what would happen if someone were to do that while they were under a gas attack. The thought leaves my stomach churning, and I try to distract myself by paying attention to what he's reading.

The rats here are the size of cats, so big that none of us decide to fight with them. They steal our rations and spread disease to whoever dares to take the chance of eating their freshly nibbled food, our food. We are left with no choice though, it's either that or we die from starvation. Sometimes, I can feel their grisly hair rubbing against us in the night, making me freeze up in fear. I have never like animals. Some guys decide to make a game out of it, by seeing who can catch the most rats. They never catch enough though, no one wins.

I feel myself being to freeze up as another teacher makes the rounds with the duster. It was as if what I was writing was taking shape in real life. It leaves us with a ticklish and weird feeling, causing us all to scoot up a little bit more forward. I turn to one of my friends, and we both cover our ears just as another teacher comes by, banging on the tables with big wooden blocks. It would be all right if we weren't directly below the table, but we are, and there's nothing we can do about it.

The hours drag on, leaving room for the ugly thoughts that flow through my head. I begin to feel an ache in my heart, missing my wife and daughter dearly. Occasionally, the pressure gets so intense, and the sounds become so vivid, that we start to go insane. What if I die? What if my life ends right here at this very moment, in the midst of all the bombshells and gunshots? To pass time, I think of my family. I recall their beautiful faces and all of our happy memories. I begin to question why I made this decision to just throw my life away. Why didn't I realize that I was not the man for this job sooner? This is too much stress for one man to handle. Sometimes I can't help at all. And when those times come, I freeze up and begin to act like a robot. No feelings, no emotions. Just doing my job.

Why am I choosing to write about this sort of stuff? After each pause, Mr. Southworth will read from a book written from the perspective of our current case study. He will ask us questions for which we then have to write our answers, from a point of view from someone there. Technically, Mr. Southworth's last question didn't deal with the medical aspect of the war. For some reason I felt I needed to write about it. Maybe it was because I too felt for this made up character and his daughter and wife. Maybe I wanted him to have a very happy ending, in which he would be reunited with them and they would all live happily ever after. Perhaps that's better saved for creative writing class, for now I'm in history and he was just a character.

The fear in which I lie can never be eliminated. How can you ignore the constant, rapid heartbeat in your chest? How can you ignore the sound of bombs being blown up, or the panic in each scream? How can you ignore the fact that this may be your last breath? The answer- you can't. No amount of medical training or army basic training could help us get through this struggle, it was all in our hands now. My arms are lined with fingernail marks, which are one of the reasons I'm still a bit sane. Whenever I feel my head begin to crumble under all the weight and pressure, I dig my nails into my skin, to remind me that I'm still alive and breathing. To remind myself that if I want to make it out of this war alive, I need to be able to function. Receiving letters from my Buddy Al is one of the only other things keeping me sane. I'm his role model, and boy does it make me feel great sometimes. But his newest letter tells me he's going to join, and all the happiness I once contained is emptied out of me. He is not as strong as me, and if I can barely handle it? He is setting himself up for failure. He will be beaten down by the stress and all the noises. Another body is shoved into my hands and I close my eyes as I settle it onto to the ground gently. I open them and look down, inspecting the injury. A man lays in front of me, his hair caked with sweat and mud. One of his arms has been shot off, its open wound bleeding profusely. I freeze up momentarily then get to work, knowing I have to give it my all in order to keep this man alive.

Blocks slap against the table, louder and harder this time. The speakers on the wall still projecting the soundtrack of panicked scream and shots, my heart racing with each passing second. Everyone else only seems to have half a page of answers written down, whereas I have almost three. Mr. Southworth finishes reading from the book and then everyone stops talking. All of our pencils fall to our notebooks, and we eagerly begin to stretch our legs. The speakers come to a halt and the whole room grows silent. The simulation is over, off to PE.

.   .   .

MACKENZIE PLIESKATT HAS BEEN WRITING FOR MORE THAN FOUR YEARS AND AIMS TO PUBLISH HER OWN BOOK SOON. IN ADDITION TO BEING AN AVID READER, SHE ENJOYS SPENDING TIME WITH HER DOGS AND RIDING DRESSAGE. YOU CAN ALSO FIND MACKENZIE BEHIND THE LENS OF HER CAMERA IN HER TRAVELS.

Kissing a Pig
By Emily Wilson

I had no idea when I started my credential program that the highlight of my teaching career would be trying to kiss a two-hundred-pound pig in front of the entire student body

When I got into teaching at twenty-two, I fancied myself a young Robin Williams in _Dead Poets Society_. I wanted to effect real, dramatic, fantastic change in my students. I wanted to wax poetic about Walt Whitman and inspire youngsters to become writers. Never mind that I was a young woman from a privileged background teaching at an economically disadvantaged high school. We had the county's highest number of students on free and reduced lunch; no one knew who the fuck Whitman was, or cared. These kids had bigger problems than those prep school movie boys. If I had been stuck in movie mode, channeling Michelle Pfeiffer in _Dangerous Minds_ might have helped me more in my early years as an educator.

Regardless of their economic background, or mine for that

matter, I quickly fell in love with teaching. At the end of my first month of teaching, I was ecstatic at the realization that in addition to loving what I was doing, I was getting paid to do so. It was a first-year teacher's salary in California, so it wasn't stretching far, but still. Someone was paying me to do this.

The reality was better than the movies. My kids were funny and smart and kept me on my toes. The days went by quickly because I was working my ass off to make lesson plans that were relevant to my student's experiences. Between Gatsby and *The Crucible* and what felt like grading endless essays, the time in the classroom in front of kids was even more rewarding than I thought it would be. I could see the light turn on in their eyes when something finally clicked. My students were learning because I was teaching them. It was phenomenal.

By my second or third year, I found my groove when I became one of *those teachers*. You know the ones. The ones who are always on stage, making an ass of themselves, trying to get the kids to laugh and participate. There were so many amazing teachers at my school, and I knew I would never be the "best" teacher. I didn't need that title or that kind of self-importance. Instead, I opted for trying my hardest and being active on campus instead. The memories we carry from childhood are formed on the playground, in the halls between classes, at lunch, and in the auditorium. Not in the classroom, despite what Hollywood might want us to believe.

For the sake of those memories, I choreographed and planned an airband routine to Three MCs and One DJ. I sang karaoke in front of the entire student body. I took countless pies to the face. I stayed late into the night at school to help build homecoming floats for students, even though I had zero upper body strength and none of us knew how to wield an electric drill. I chased a freshman pole vaulter for a week to help him get his sprint speed up. I volunteered for the dunk tank at the school carnival. I learned to hula dance as a part of a student/teacher dance performance. I helped a student design (and use my whiteboard) to ask his friend to the homecoming dance. I sang Disney songs for an ASB music video. I even played in a teacher basketball game, despite my lack of athletic ability.

One of my all-time favorite memories teaching was when a senior asked me to throw out the first pitch at his varsity baseball game. Despite my aforementioned noodle arms, I happily said yes first and worried later. I confessed that I probably wouldn't be any good, but that I was happy to do it. He just smiled and said he'd bring his glove and a ball the next day to class. And for the rest of the week during homeroom, we played catch. He taught me how to grip the ball, the right way to stand, and how to make sure I threw it far enough to make it over home plate.

Those were the things that made teaching for me. Those were the moments I lived for. Those are the memories I cherish now that I'm not teaching anymore. Not the intricate lessons I designed in the classroom, not the long discussions about *Madame Bovary*, but showing up for my kids. I was willing to just about anything they asked me to.

And then came the pig.

It was all for a fundraiser at school; I don't even remember what it was for, honestly. I remember getting a bucket in my classroom and telling kids to donate if they were able. I knew the best performing class's reward was watching their teacher kiss a pig. The thought was delightfully hilarious at the time, but I didn't think anything of it. Once I found out that teachers were actively telling their students not to donate because they didn't want to kiss the pig, my tune changed. I leaned into it. Hard. I told the students that I thought pigs were cute. That I loved the movie *Charlotte's Web* as a kid because I thought Wilbur was adorable. I wanted to *be* Fern.

Considering I was the volunteer club advisor, I spent a lot of time talking about the spirit of donating. That it wasn't about how much you could give, or how much you have. That giving freely is one of the most human things that we could do. That empathy was our greatest superpower. I'm pretty sure I even sang (terribly) at my kids. Matter of fact, I know I did. It was my old cheer routine from when I was in high school. I did whatever I could. I worked that muscle I'd been flexing for years. Like my work husband/ASB advisor/history teacher extraordinaire would say, "I'd teach a lesson standing on my head while wearing a Santa suit if I thought it would help them learn something." That was my version of standing on my head.

The kids ate it up. They took their cue from me, on how much I seemed to care about this fundraiser. My students ended up donating more than any other we'd had that year. It was astonishing, how much they were able to contribute. Which of course meant that I would have to plant a smacker on some bovine lips.

I was so damn proud of my kids; it took my breath away.

It was like that scene in The Grinch; my heart grew three sizes knowing how generous my kids were. My little class of juniors had helped our school raise the most money it had in over a decade. *My kids.* Those were my babies that did that wonderful, selfless thing. Even if it the root of it was based on wanting to watch me do something stupid, they chose to give. To be a part of something bigger. It was better than the whole Professor Keating fantasy because it was authentic to my students, my school, and to my teachings. If kissing a pig would show them how proud I was of them, I was happy to do it. I would have kissed ten pigs for them. Dozens. Hundreds.

When the day of the fated kiss came, the lights were low in the gymnasium, and the seats were packed with students. The students from 4-H had given the audience the option of paramours for me: the squeaky-clean adorable piglet, or the two hundred pound Bubba who looked as though he hadn't had a bath in a year. The reckless part of my brain laughed, knowing the kids would love the big guy. That it would make a better show, and that the kids would be laughing about it for a week. I didn't think about hygiene, or about the fact that it outweighed me by almost eighty pounds. All I thought about was the kids. This was gonna be a hit. I cheered along with my students as they heavily rooted for Bubba. We were all in on this together. I clapped as they put the small little babe away and let the big guy out. I was up.

Five minutes later, I was running around a gymnasium floor, chasing Bubba and trying to get him to kiss me. The 4-H kids eventually had to trap the pig because I was such a spaz on the floor that I couldn't get near it. It ran faster than me. There was no doubt that I looked like the biggest idiot ever. I'd made a reputation for myself as the teacher that would do anything for her kids, no matter how dumb I looked, no matter how stupid or gross it was.

And it was true. I would have done anything for my students.

I kissed that pig, and I loved every bit of it.

EMILY WILSON IS A FORMER HIGH SCHOOL ENGLISH TEACHER AND CURRENT MOTHER OF DRAGONS. SHE IS A NOVELIST, FREELANCE EDITOR/COPYWRITER, AND COMMISSIONED ARTIST. SHE HAS AN MASTER'S IN AMERICAN LITERATURE, WHICH HAS NOT HELPED HER ONE BIT IN RAISING TINY HUMANS, BUT INTRODUCED HER TO A FEW GOOD BOOKS. EMILY HAS LIVED IN SAN DIEGO FOR SO LONG THAT, AT THIS POINT, SHE IS MOSTLY MADE OF BURRITOS AND SAND.

31

Perfect Isn't Perfect and Other Things I Learned in School
By Laurie Walker

I always wanted to be a teacher.

When I was a very little girl I would line up my stuffed animals as though in a classroom and make them listen to me. They were excellent students. Except for the seal, but everyone knows seals are trouble makers. I would give assignments, answer questions, put the seal in time out, and grade papers. I was very dedicated. I was making a difference in those stuffie's lives.

By first grade I was the obnoxious kid who wanted to be "in charge" when the teacher left the room. Yes, my first-grade teacher left us alone in the room. It was the 70s, for the love. Anyway, I knew I was both perfectly suited for the job and ultimately more mature than every other person available.

I'm sure I was a damn delight.

It went on like that through elementary school. When my friends and I played school, I was *always* the teacher.

Throughout my whole life I loved the beginning of every school year.

I was amped up by the smell of new pencils and erasers, thrilled by not yet doodled on Pee-Chees, by sharp crayons, and by brand spanking new shoes. I adored the fresh possibilities found in blank paper and seating charts. I still get giddy over school supply sales. I can be bought for the right stack of sticky notes and colored paper clips.

I pictured becoming a teacher someday and having a creative, colorful classroom full of beautiful, bright children, all of whom adored me and hung on my every word. I would have access to the teachers' lounge and all of its mysteries, and I would be a guiding light in the educational darkness. The world would be perfect.

I would make a difference in the lives of *all* the children.

Then I grew up.

Shit happened. Like, A LOT of shit.

Without gory details, I didn't finish college. I made terrible choices. I tried to be a lot of other things besides a teacher and none of them worked out and none of them were happy and none of them were even close to perfect.

I wasn't making a difference in anyone's life.

I was a single mother of two, checking groceries on a closing shift, just trying to survive. I felt like no one's guiding light, not my own and certainly not for anyone else's child.

I applied for jobs in the school district simply because I wanted to be on the same schedule as my children when they started kindergarten and was blessed to be hired as a para educator, a fancy name for a teacher's aide. I had never earned my degree, but in those days you didn't need one to assist. You needed a high school diploma, common sense, and the ability to relate to kids.

Check, check, check.

My first classroom wasn't bright and shiny with sweet second or third graders eager to please and thirsty for knowledge. It was not the picture perfect image I had as a child. I went to work in an alternative high school with students aged fourteen to twenty who couldn't care less about my dream to make a difference in their lives.

The kids I worked with came from all different directions. Most didn't want to be there. Some were there under court order. Some had been kicked out of every other school and this was their last shot. Some just didn't fit in anywhere else. Ninety percent of them were significantly behind in their classes. Thirty percent were, in some way, affected by drugs and/or alcohol abuse. Some were homeless. The graduation rate hovered around forty percent, but that was difficult to track because we never had the same kids for an entire school year.

In my first week I met a fourteen-year old student whose mother had passed away from cancer, his father was nowhere to be found, and his grandmother, his only remaining relative and caregiver, was also dying of cancer. While I was in the bathroom broken-hearted and ugly crying, my coworkers were setting up a betting pool on how fast I'd burn out.

The longest any of them gave me was ninety days.

I was there seven years.

Those cheaters never paid up on that bet either.

In the course of that time I was an assistant to three different teachers, an unofficial counselor to both students and parents, unofficial registrar/administrative assistant/errand runner, and a student teacher (I did a practicum class when I attempted to go back to school). I held the hands of pregnant teenage girls while they prepared to make one of the most important decisions of their lives. More than once I was backed into a literal corner by a violent student only to look into his eyes and see he was the one really and truly trapped. He had lived a life where fear and violence was his only way forward; he just needed help to find a different path. Once I stood with a fifteen-year-old boy while he was handcuffed by police serving a warrant for his arrest at school. He tried to look tough, but he was really just a scared kid who needed someone, anyone, to tell him it was going to be okay and he could choose to make his life right again.

And, in one school year alone, I grieved the tragedies of five young people lost to five drug- or alcohol-related accidents.

The number of times I went home crying and frustrated overwhelmingly outweighed the times I went home feeling like I'd made some kind of positive difference in the lives of these kids. I broke into a million pieces so many times I lost count. I became, alternately, jaded and annoyingly idealistic in my need to save them all.

I learned many lessons in those seven years:

I learned how to spot a kid high on drugs.

I learned how to be tough when I needed to be and how to back down when it was safer and necessary for both the student and myself.

I learned when not to wear my staff ID on a lanyard around my neck because it could be used to choke me out. Seriously.

I learned how to be compassionate to a child who had never known love in any healthy form.

I learned that Child Protective Services doesn't always protect.

I learned that there are parents who actually quit on their kids.

I learned that there are parents who will do anything, give up everything, for their kids and NEVER quit.

I learned that a parent's bad choice has a lifelong impact on a child.

I learned that kids who make bad decisions sometimes have really good parents who are trying their very best.

I learned that very good kids sometimes make really bad decisions.

And I learned that a good teacher can be more than just an educator. She can be a lifeline.

I really don't remember a lot about the curriculum we taught in those seven years. I don't remember the course names or what our grading policies were.

What I remember is the smile on a student's face when he finally passed a class for the first time in a year and was driven to do it again and again until he graduated.

I remember comforting the best friend of a student who had died and how I admired the tattoo he got in honor of a boy who was more brother to him than friend. How we sat and cried together over that boy who never saw the end of his teenage years. How we talked about the changes he, the survivor, would make in his life so he could truly *live* in tribute.

I remember a student calling me on the phone in the middle of a family crisis, then hanging up. I was unable to find or help her. Four months went by when I knew nothing of what happened to her, until one day she just walked into our classroom again. Safe.

I remember a parent calling me once a week to talk about her son because she just didn't know what else to do to help him; she wanted to give up. She would talk for thirty minutes until she had talked herself around to a next step. She just needed someone to listen who also cared about her son because every other person in their lives had given up on him.

I remember getting into countless arguments with countless educators and administrators about what was more important: the education or the well being of the student. For me, they went hand in hand. A child could not learn if she didn't feel safe and loved. It didn't matter if she was five or fifteen.

My job ended because of state budget cuts. It was sad, and I was sorry to lose my connection to a very special group of kids. They were not little, cute, or shiny. They were hard and complicated. They were not excited, eager children in a perfect, colorful classroom. They were broken and hurting and needy.

Instead of hanging on to my every word, I listened to them. Instead of me being in charge of it all, they formed a world I fit into where I fought for something more important than supplies and seating charts.

Teaching didn't turn out to be even remotely what I expected it to be. Instead of being idyllic it was complicated and messy.

But, in the end, it was perfect.

Perfect for me because I thought my dream of teaching was out of my reach.

Perfect for me who was damaged and rough and could relate so much to kids who were the same. We fit together. It wasn't easy or rosy, like my childhood classroom of stuffies, but we fit. At the end of it all I'm not sure who had the greater impact on whom.

Perfect because the bright, shiny image I had carried around about what I thought being a teacher meant was never real anyway. Every child has edges, no matter what they appear to be, and every teacher has something to learn no matter how much she thinks she knows.

I will never forget those kids. I will never forget the hands I was fortunate enough to hold or the tears I cried for each of those kids. I will never forget the achievements they celebrated and the joy they shared with me.

For a few moments they were mine, and they were just perfect.

LAURI WALKER IS WIFE TO ONE HANDSOME MAN AND, MAMA TO FOUR KIDS WHO'VE MANAGED GENIUS STATUS DESPITE BEING RAISED ON CHICKEN NUGGETS AND TAKEOUT. SHE'S THE COACH'S WIFE, A SPORTS MAMA, AND HER CAR SMELLS LIKE BASEBALL CLEATS NO MATTER HOW HARD SHE TRIES. LAURI HAS HER OWN BLOG AT MAMA NEEDS A NAP AND CONTRIBUTES TO THAT'S INAPPROPRIATE AND FILTER FREE PARENTS. SHE HAS ALSO APPEARED ON PERFECTION PENDING, SCARY MOMMY, AND GROWN AND FLOWN, AMONG OTHERS. YOU CAN FIND HER ON FACEBOOK, TWITTER, AND INSTAGRAM.

32

Infraction Abreast
By AK Turner

My husband and I decided long ago that travel would be as much a part of our children's education as any sort of formal schooling. We wanted to expose them to as many cultures as possible. They'd be worldly but humble. Global citizens of the twenty-first century. They'd develop a broad range of interests and tastes. We would not allow them to live in a cultural vacuum and survive on chicken nuggets and French fries.

We had the best of intentions.

By the time they were ten, my girls had traveled to Australia, Brazil, Spain, Canada, Ireland, Mexico, and Scotland. Were they worldly? Yes. But they'd also spent their lives surviving on chicken nuggets and French fries in each of those countries. Side note: chicken nuggets and French fries are remarkably similar the world over.

Though the bulk of our travels took place during school breaks, there were plenty of trips which necessitated withdrawing them from our local public elementary.I am wildly successful in my role as parent when my kids are being educated by other people. I can hand my kids off to teachers like nobody's business. I can drop them off curbside at the school on time, well rested, appropriately fed, with sharpened number two pencils and signed permission slips. I give my kids over to public education like a boss.

When *I* am the responsible party—when I'm homeschooling or world schooling or remote schooling, my efforts amount to a series of failures and emotional scarring for all parties involved.

Sometimes I fail in small ways, like my inability to teach Common Core math. I end up reverting to good old-fashioned long division, which I never thought I'd think of fondly, but after you've failed at teaching Common Core math and your kids are crying as if you've been waterboarding them, teaching long division feels positively joyful.

This particular failure took place in the Amazon. Not the online retailer that's soon to take over the world, the actual rainforest that's slowly dying because humans are assholes. This was part of a two-month trek in Brazil. In addition to long division, we learned just how bad the human body can smell in a tropical environment with no running water. If you homeschool or worldschool, I do not recommend adding this particular lesson to your curriculum.

When it comes to fractions, I fail hard. But truthfully, I can think of no instance in my adult life when I've had to multiply fractions. Why is this even a thing? In the grocery store, when calculating cost or nutritional value, I have never had to think to myself, *Well, I'll just multiply 5/6ths x 2/31sts and Bob's your uncle!*

The only benefit of teaching fraction multiplication is recognizing the creative genius behind the story problems that couch the actual math.

If a pallet of donuts is 3,400 sprinkled and 2,900 glazed, and Samantha consumes 8/29ths of the glazed donuts and 7/36ths of the sprinkled donuts, and Billy eats 5/12ths of the sprinkled and 89/156ths of the glazed, who will die first?

It's much more fun to say "screw the math" and instead use your environment as the education itself.

For instance, at a koala hospital in Australia, we learned that the number one ailment to koalas is chlamydia (they're randy little buggers).

In Spain I taught my daughters that despite what my in-laws might call it, flamenco dancing in no way involves flamingoes.

In Scotland we learned about traditional Highland games, which as far as I can tell involves very large men in kilts moving massive objects around and trying not to drop any of those objects on spectators.

I'm fairly certain that all of this valuable knowledge will serve my children well.

There are times when I need a break, because when we travel I am with my children every hour of every day. There are no superhuman teachers to hand them off to, no babysitters to book for a few hours. So my husband and I scheduled massages to give ourselves a parenting/teaching break during a week on Thailand's island of Koh Phangan.

We were 8/29ths sure that our daughters were old enough to keep themselves alive with no parental supervision.

"Should we just go for the regular Thai massage?" Mike asked as we looked at the massage menu.

Massage menus are substantial. I'm sure there are some establishments with options like crotch massage or love rub, but the choices at cootie-free parlors fall more along the lines of Thai massage, coconut oil massage, or neck and back massage, all of which I've tried.

"We could try their signature massage," I suggested. "It's two hours long."

The previous day of travel to reach Koh Phangan had involved a grueling itinerary: a one hour taxi ride, five hour bus ride, two hour wait, one hour bus ride, fifteen minute trolley ride, four hour ferry ride (on which ferry there was no alcohol available for purchase), and a final thirty minutes in a tuk-tuk. A tuk-tuk is sort of like an open air taxi. Depending on traffic, it could also be referred to as "death bucket."

We'd earned a two-hour massage.

I had no reason to fear the massage. I'd had plenty of Thai massages. A row of massage beds sat on a raised, outdoor platform. It wasn't as if we were being led into a windowless room that reeked of money laundering and bodily fluids. The women taking charge of us were sturdily in their fifties. They looked like the type of women who would never dream of jaywalking or tracking dirt across a freshly cleaned floor. They were my kind of people.

"I'm just wearing my swim shorts," Mike whispered anxiously as we were led to our side-by-side massage beds.

"So what?"

"So I feel like I should have underwear on underneath or something."

"Oh, stop worrying," I chided. "I'm sure it will be fine."

I had my swimsuit on as well, and I'd learned from previous massages that this was a good way to go. When I wore regular clothes, I was told to strip down to my underwear. This is more than one wears for a massage in the States (usually nothing) but those massages take place in rooms with doors that close, not on beachfront raised platforms for all the world to see. If I had to choose whether to be on display in my bathing suit or underwear, I'd choose bathing suit. Because even though I should have updated my bathing suit twelve pounds ago, my underwear has holes in it.

I'm not proud.

A few minutes later I was face down, my masseuse straddling my back. Thais have no trepidation about maneuvering around underwear *or* swimsuit bottoms, and my masseuse at times pulled my suit lower for better access to my buttocks, thereby also exposing a healthy portion of my butt crack.

Most people who get embarrassed at the thought of revealing their butt crack don't realize that they're putting it on display every time they crouch down in their low-rise jeans. Seriously, far more people have probably seen your butt crack than you realize. And nobody cares about anybody else's ass envelope anyway.

When she was done with the buttock region, my masseuse attempted to put my suit bottoms back in their rightful place. Unfortunately she overcompensated and ended up giving me a tremendous wedgie.

It took me back to my childhood.

My reverie broke when she said, "I take off," and began untying my bikini top.

"Oh. Um. Okay," I said.

I glanced over at Mike then to see that his swim shorts were gone, but in their place he'd donned a disposable black piece of crotchwear they'd provided. It couldn't really be described as underwear. More like a penis wrap.

He undoubtedly wished he'd followed his instincts and donned a pair of underwear to avoid having to wear what resembled, to me, a flimsy, mesh, dick purse.

I returned my attention to my own situation. In addition to my grand wedgie, I was now topless. On the other hand, I didn't really mind the removal of my bikini top, as I was face down and this gave my masseuse better access to massaging my back.

The Thais have it figured out. Massage is less about your thumbs and more about leveraging your body weight. In this way, she applied pressure with her forearms and legs onto all parts of my body. It's the type of pressure that I imagine John Mellencamp singing about back when he still felt his inner Cougar. It hurts. So. Good.

While still face down, she pulled my arms back behind me, then pulled up so that my chest raised off the mat. I was like a figurehead carved at the prow of a ship, back arched and breasts dangling. I sort of cared, but was more preoccupied with whether or not my shoulders were going to dislocate from their sockets. Because if they did, I surely would not have the strength to reach back around to tie my bikini top. That could be problematic, and I didn't know if my husband would be game to help me. Not only was his attention overwhelmed by his package in a dick purse, but he was also in the process of having his own shoulders dislocated.

When she lowered me back to the mat, I was fairly certain that I still had full use of my arms.

"Turn over," she commanded.

I did so, fully expecting her to put a sheet over my body and chest, but instead she put a small towel over my crotch area. I had the bathing suit bottoms on, so didn't think this entirely necessary. Then again, how long had it been since I'd properly groomed? What if I had tufts of pubic hair peeking out to say hello? Was that why she was using the precious real estate of the towel to cover my crotch, leaving my dirty pillows exposed and sagging toward their respective armpits?

The massage continued and I tried not to think of my fun bags on display. This worked well as she massaged my legs and arms. But then she moved to the stomach.

I can think of many reasons why a full body massage should not necessarily include the full body. And many of those reasons have to do with the stomach. It's ticklish. It raises insecurities about the skin-to-fat-to-muscle ratio of the stomach. It is precariously placed above the crotch and below the breasts. All of these things should qualify this particular area as off limits during a massage. Just like you don't want your nostrils or your knee-pits or your anus massaged, you don't want your stomach massaged.

Unless you *do* want your anus massaged, but this isn't that type of story.

I was relieved when the stomach massage ended. Until she began the boob massage. At which point I would have paid her extra to return to the stomach massage.

Maybe that was a slip up.

Perhaps she accidentally *brushed my breasts with each of her hands at the same time in a motion that clearly resembled massage.*

Surely that was the case. Surely this wasn't...

But there it was again.

Lying on my back, eyes closed, the masseuse perched above my head. She used the full range of motion, both hands with fingers spread wide, to fully massage my bitties.

Wait... what???

It was so surreal that I almost chuckled. And then I realized that because of that, I had a smirk on my face, which might be interpreted as a smile.

Oh, fuck. Now she's going to think I'm enjoying this!

So I began frowning, and then I was pretty sure I just looked angry. I wasn't angry. I was just shocked. And uncomfortable to have a Thai woman in her fifties massaging my boobs. Not that my discomfort was related to the fact that she was Thai or a woman or in her fifties. I would have felt the same discomfort if anyone massaged my knockers. If my husband, in the heat of passion, began fondling my boobs in any manner similar to that massage, I would have burst out laughing and asked him what the hell he was doing. Because no one can ruin a moment quite like I can.

Instead, I did what most women do when they're uncomfortable with how they're being touched. I went stock-still and waited it out, thinking of all the better ways I'd react if it ever happened again.

The entire boob portion of the two-hour massage could not have lasted more than twenty seconds. But those were twenty weird-ass seconds.

When the massage was over we drank tea and I said an awkward *khob-khun-kha* (thank you) to my masseuse. Mike and I walked back to our room to check on our neglected children.

"What did you think of the signature massage?" he asked.

"She massaged my boobs."

"What? She did? And I missed it?"

"She full-on massaged my boobs. There was no mistaking it."

"Oh, man," he said. This news seemed to have made his day.

"Did you get *your* chest massaged?" I asked. "Tell me you had to suffer through some awkward pec-fondling."

"Nope. Nothing like that."

"So unfair," I said. Because somehow it would have made me feel better to know that my husband had been experiencing equal levels of discomfort. Isn't that what marriage is all about?

Then again, he did have to suffer the indignity of the schlong-sarong.

We headed back to our worldly-but-nugget-addicted children and I thought about the rest of our trip. We had another month to go before we'd return to the United States, where I could once again hand my children over to those superhuman beings called "teachers," those curious creatures who could somehow explain math to my children without making them cry. Because my own efforts were falling short.

Perhaps I just needed to liven up the content:

Question: If a wedgie causes Amanda 8/156ths of discomfort and a boob massage makes her feel 921/12ths weird, what are the chances she will *never again* pay someone to fondle her mammaries?

Answer: One hundred percent.

AK TURNER IS THE *NEW YORK TIMES* BESTSELLING AUTHOR OF *THE VAGABONDING WITH KIDS* SERIES AS WELL AS *THIS LITTLE PIGGY WENT TO THE LIQUOR STORE, MOMMY HAD A LITTLE FLASK,* AND *HAIR OF THE CORN DOG.* FOLLOW HER DIGITAL NOMAD FAMILY ADVENTURES AT YOUTUBE: WHAT WOULD TURNERS DO? NO BOOB SHOTS OR DICK PICS, PROMISE. LEARN MORE AT AKTURNER.COM.

33

Being a Teacher Doesn't Make Me a Better Mother (but Being a
Mother Makes me a Better Teacher)
By Julia Arnold

A good friend of mine once made the comment, "I think I'd be a better mom if I had been a teacher first." As a teacher and a mother, it made me think. I understand the sentiment behind the theory: that working with children professionally would give you a solid understanding of young people, their development, their personalities, their brains. Perhaps it would also help when figuring out a disciplinary system at home [that actually works] and lay the foundation for the organization required in daily life with children. Basically, the premise is that the skills learned in the classroom would apply to life at home.

There might be some truth in it. However, having been a teacher prior to having children of my own, I can say that nothing in the classroom truly prepared me for motherhood. Motherhood, however, has had a profound impact on how I work with children and families on a professional level.

Fresh out of college and graduate school, degree in hand, I was ready (*so, so* ready) to educate and connect on a deep level with all the wonderful young people in our country! I was determined to work with even the most challenging high school students, to be firm but fair. The Mary Poppins of the modern-day education system. I imagined I would be that fun, friendly teacher who they all loved and who taught them both academic and life lessons. I cringe with embarrassment at the memory of being energized by Michelle Pfeiffer's character as a teacher in a tough inner city school who inspired troubled students in the movie *Dangerous Minds*. *I will be exactly like her!* I thought, if just given the chance.

My teaching license is in learning disabilities, and my undergraduate degree is in English literature. Combine the two, and *boom!*— I was the ideal candidate for a job teaching high school English to students with dyslexia, ADHD, dysgraphia, and other learning disorders and challenges. I was thrilled to get that very first full-time job, a milestone synonymous with being a truly independent adult, but I was also full of new-teacher nerves. *Will they eat me alive?* I wondered, lying in bed at night, staring at the ceiling in the weeks leading up to the first day of school. Other concerns still make my stomach churn when I remember them: *Will they like me? Will I be able to actually, like, teach them anything?* I was only twenty-three at the time—practically a child myself—and looking back, I was unbearably young to take on such a large task. I realized that I would no longer just be responsible for myself, but for dozens of teenagers. *Yikes.*

And though that job was harder than I could have even imagined during those sleepless nights, with many ups and downs, I grew to love it and, honestly, I became quite good at it. Despite the challenges, it was a dream job for me. The years I taught in a special education classroom transformed my life in many ways, perhaps the greatest of which was that I had the privilege of watching students grow in their abilities and their confidence and move on to happier, more successful school and life experiences after I worked with them.

But here's the thing I didn't fully understand until exactly eight and a half years ago when my first child was born: each of the students I would meet that first year and in the years following would be someone's child. Yes, of course I knew that on a basic level. They came from *somewhere*, obviously. However, I know now that we can not fully comprehend in our hearts what each and every child means to their parents before we have them ourselves.

Only parents know in their gut the feeling of anticipating a baby for nine months, eagerly awaiting their birth and daydreaming incessantly about what their lives would be like together as that baby grew. If it's a boy, we wonder, will we name him after Uncle Hank and take him fishing in the summer up north? Will he have his dad's blue-green eyes and my generous spattering of freckles? Or, if it's a little girl, will she have a head of soft, dark hair from day one? Will she like the ocean and running and animals as much as I do?

We all know that the wide-eyed, dreamy pregnancy stage occupies just the tiniest tip of the iceberg, a blip in our journey as parents. The constant pull on our heads and hearts only intensifies after our babies are born. Our deep-seated instinct to protect our offspring at all costs is intense. Despite the torturous labors we endure, the inhumane sleepless nights that make us deliriously unlike our pre-child selves, and the freedom we give up when we have babies, we all know it is worth it. We will guard these babies with our lives.

As they grow, these small people present us with new joys and challenges on a daily basis. Often it is the challenges, unfortunately, that we focus on—that hijack our brains at night after a long day. The toddler who only eats yogurt and fish sticks. The preschooler who cries every time he has to separate from his mother. The kindergartener who still wets the bed or sucks her thumb. The worry is exhausting. All of it. Yet, still, we experience that fierce, protective love as they inevitably grow and we eventually send them off to school each day. That insomnia that keeps us up, our worries spinning in our brains: *Are they making friends? Are they happy? Am I being strict enough? Am I being too strict?* I doubt it ever goes away.

FAST FORWARD ABOUT twelve or thirteen years from that naive first year of teaching, and how has parenthood, this all-encompassing chapter in my life, affected me as a teacher?

First, I now realize I rarely thought too much about how the parents of my students were feeling. On a basic level, I understood that the parents loved their children and were even going so far as to make sacrifices to send them to an expensive, specialized school to help improve those crucial reading and writing skills. No one dreams of or prepares for having a child with special needs and the extra funds that may be required to support them as they grow. I could sense their worry during conferences, and I tried to be positive and supportive. I received and dutifully responded to all of the concerned emails over the years. I had empathy for these families, certainly. But I was far more focused on the children than the adults.

Now I know just how much each child matters to each family, and how dependent the family's overall well-being is on the happiness of each child. The expression, "You're only as happy as your least happy child" is startlingly accurate. Many of these families were struggling or in crisis. Their high schoolers—some as old as eighteen—were still learning to read, spell, and write. Did I have compassion for them? Of course. Could I have had even more? Yes, though perhaps not until I had experienced the intense highs and lows of motherhood for myself.

I now operate as a private tutor so I can work with children and teens around my own family's busy schedule as well as my freelance career. My conversations with my tutoring clients' parents have changed. Now I always start with: "Tell me about your child. You know them best. I want to hear all about them!" And I mean it. The relief a parent expresses at such a nonjudgmental interest in their child is palpable. Too often as parents we focus on the negatives and challenges that we are currently experiencing with our children—a call from the teacher about disruptive classroom behavior, a cruel remark made on the playground, the hurt our children feel if they don't make the team—so I think it's vital to get parents talking and thinking about all the good that's inside their children. That's where we start.

I feel at this point, I have truly seen it all. I have taught dozens—maybe hundreds—of students, which provides me with a wide berth of experience, but so much more important—I have children of my own. My family has our own set of needs, challenges, and strengths—just like all of yours. Some days and weeks, the challenges weigh heavily upon my husband and me. To the point of that all-encompassing, heavy worry that only parents know. The sleepless nights of newborn days can return. Our lives are not always what we dreamed of during those 9 months of gestation. Other days with our children, fortunately, are wonderful; these are the days our children shine brightly, we feel content with our place in the world, and we are reminded of the happiness our family is so grateful to enjoy. Those times sustain us.

Now I come to each tutoring session and each meeting with this understanding. I can't part with it. It's there, with me, each and every session. It stays with me when I'm planning a lesson or setting goals or trying to excite my students. It's there when I talk to parents, offering support and encouragement.

So while I might have been a decent teacher before having kids, I feel like I am a much, much better teacher—and listener and ally—for the families I work with now that I'm a mom. I can't say being a teacher made me a better mom—I'm quite imperfect at it, frankly—but I can unequivocally say that being a mom has made me a better teacher.

JULIA ARNOLD IS A FREELANCE WRITER AND READING TUTOR BASED IN MINNESOTA. THIS IS HER FIFTH ANTHOLOGY. SHE LOVES WRITING ABOUT PARENTHOOD, EDUCATION, ANIMALS, AND NONPROFITS. SHE IS MARRIED TO HER COLLEGE SWEETHEART AND HAS TWO GREAT KIDS.

34

Speak Softly and Carry a Big Stick
By Amy Rosenberg

Nakamura Sensei had a deep tan, a neatly trimmed mustache and the confidence of a much younger, much taller man. He seemed formidable to me, as a twenty-two-year-old American woman, fresh from college and new to Japan. I had come to Japan to teach English in a rotation of schools on an idyllic Pacific island. The first two Japanese words I learned were spider and earthquake because my first day on the island, driving to my apartment, I got whiplash doing double-takes as I caught sight of one enormous spider after the next after the next hanging in webs stretched between palm trees along the highway. And there was a sizable earthquake on day two of my tenure there.

Mainly I taught in the high school in the tiny city where I lived but I also traveled all around the island assisting at middle schools, some where there was only one student in a class. No matter how tiny the village, each had its own school. And so I white-knuckled rides over mountains, through ridiculously long tunnels and all over this spider-infested island to teach with a wide variety of wonderful Senseis.

Most of the teachers were confident in their English abilities, even though I often couldn't understand a word they said. Nakamura Sensei was no different in this regard. "Emily-san," he would say to me (even though my name is Amy), "read this page please." I would stare at him, having no idea what he wanted me to do until he pointed at the textbook. Sometimes he brought me to the language lab and asked me to record passages from the textbook while he sat next to me smoking. As a guest in a country where politeness reigns supreme, I didn't want to be rude. I was too intimidated to ask someone not to smoke around me. Sitting next to people smoking was my life as an English Teacher in Japan for a year.

Nakamura was different to say the least. I appreciated his panache. He wasn't anything like the other teachers in our little high school in the middle of the ocean on tropical Amami Oshima; he wasn't like any teachers I'd come across in Japan for that matter. Most teachers were imported from the mainland and seemed to have perfect hair, perfect clothes, and perfect manners. In this way they modeled for the kids how to become perfect citizens. But Nakamura was an islander and reminded me vaguely of a soap opera star. His shirt was always unbuttoned one button too many, revealing his undershirt. His hair was curly and a little unruly. And then there was that mustache; I've never seen another Japanese man with a mustache outside of historic pictures from the Edo Samurai period. A samurai with no facial hair would have been teased. But a school-teacher in 1995 could get fired for having a mustache. Being the most honored profession in Japan, teachers comport themselves with great care, speaking in an incredibly robotic manner using no facial expressions and revealing no personality underneath their words. Nakamura's face was an open book; you could always tell if he was pleased ... or angry.

At the beginning of my short tenure as an English teacher in Japan, I was so nervous and out of my element, I tried to emulate the teachers I worked with. I learned the proper greetings for entering rooms (I'm being rude), the sayings to use to begin each class (let's start—stand up—bow!), the words to end a class (let's finish). I spent countless hours reading from textbooks and listening to children trying to repeat the words they were hearing.

Once I got comfortable, however, I devised my own lessons and asked my Japanese counterparts to give me some time during each lesson to share something useful with the kids. In one such lesson I explained how in both English and Japanese languages there are four ways to convey a positive answer (yes, uh-huh, mm-hmm, and yeah). This seemed genius to me but unfortunately "yeah" sounds exactly like "no" in casual Japanese. In hindsight, I know the kids were snickering in their seats every time I said the English word "yeah" because they heard it as "no" in their native language.

I found there were many times my American communication ended up exactly backwards in the context of Japanese culture. Picture a Mom telling her kids to get out of the house because they are making too much noise. What is she doing with her hand? You know that "Shoo! Get out of here!" motion? That is exactly how you signal to a person in Japan to come over to you. (In America, to tell someone to "come here" we do this weird beckoning motion with our index finger. Ever thought about how obscene that might look to someone who's not used to it? I can't imagine in how many countries it's illegal to make the American "come here" sign with your finger.) In Japan, they make our "get out of here" motion to gesture for people to come closer. I never got used to it. Every time I saw it I thought, "You want me to get away from you? No? Come closer?" I was often like a yo-yo, fluctuating between moving towards and away from people.

With all these contradictions between Japanese and American language and culture, I shouldn't have been as surprised when laid back Nakamura Sensei turned out to be the strictest teacher I worked with. He introduced me to the popular Japanese sport known as Kendo—and not in a good way. Kendo is a martial art where you wield a sword, swinging it around and fighting with other sword-wielding people. And in order not to kill people right away when you are just learning Kendo, and probably later on when you get espe-cially good at it, people always practice with a Kendo stick. If you are curious about this sport, you can find a Kendo club just about anywhere in the United States and you can buy a pair of Kendo sticks on Amazon for thirty-five dollars!

Nakamura Sensei seemed like a cool guy. If you have ever hung out with Japanese English teachers, at least in my experience, being cool wasn't really a prerequisite. In fact, I think that's mainly true for English teachers around the globe. You have to have a certain kind of personality to become a bonafide expert in the English language and cool is not usually part of it. Really into rules? Check. A stickler for memorizing exceptions to rules? Yes. Intelligence, stamina and patience? Check. Coolness is just a unicorn-level bonus.

What I learned in Nakamura Sensei's class that year was that while a guy may come across like he is trying to be a Japanese Magnum PI, that same guy can still be the strictest, cruelest teacher in all of Japan. Nakamura Sensei taught his classes with an eight-foot Kendo stick nearby.

Initially I remember wondering if corporal punishment was legal in Japan and if anyone cared either way. I wasn't sure because I grew up in Topeka, Kansas where many things that were illegal happened anyway and as a kid I knew there was nothing I could do about it. My Topeka teachers and principals sometimes hung a paddle on the wall as a reminder of what could happen to disobedient students. So I was familiar with the concept of corporal punishment but I'd never seen a teacher crack a student over the head with a big stick! And yet that's exactly what happened in Nakamura Sensei's English class.

It was October and my first time teaching in the class with him when one of the boys refused to give an answer out loud. He stood there looking at us with a strange expression on his face. Before I knew what was happening, Nakamura held the stick out across the room and cracked the boy over the head with it. The boy rubbed his head and the class snickered. Nakamura growl-yelled at the class to shut up or he'd crack them all over the heads. In Japanese, you can get all that across with one shouted word: URUSAI. Of course, when you quietly say the same word it just means noisy. "My, the lovely birds are urusai today." Or "URUSAI!" = "Shut the hell up or I will crack you all over the head with this stick!"

I couldn't take it. I simply couldn't bear to see him beat our students but I didn't know what to do or say. I was too intimidated to stand up to him. The first time this happened, I just stood there in agony, powerless to stop him from beating the students who he deemed worthy of this kind of correction. For the record, Japan first made corporal punishment illegal in 1879. The problem is Japan had to pass similar laws, over and over again, four more times through 1945, because no one was getting the memo. Including Nakamura Sensei.

I felt terrible after class, knowing that I wasn't going to say anything to Nakamura or anyone else. I had to figure out what to do quickly because I knew that I couldn't stand to watch him beat anyone else over the head and yet I couldn't bear the thought of intervening. Caught in an impossible dilemma, I put it out of my mind until the next time I had to go to class with him about a month later.

I'll never forget that day. We stood beside each other on the wide, slightly raised platform looking out at the class of thirty kids. Some of the kids looked defiant, in spite of the punishment they would receive by way of a kendo-stick crack over the head if they did anything out of line. I stood, unsettled, one eye on the eight foot tall Kendo stick leaning against the wall and the other on Nakamura Sensei. And then it happened. One of the students spoke out of turn. Nakamura Sensei growled something angry in Japanese and headed for the stick.

Without thinking, really before I even realized what I was doing, I lunged for the stick. I reached it before he could grab it and held it tight to my body.

He looked at me, shocked. "Emily-san, please give me the stick." I ignored him. The students snickered. I was frozen in place. I clutched the stick with all of the might that my five-foot-two-inch, one-hundred-five-pound body could muster.

Nakamura Sensei did nothing. There was nothing he could do.

He resumed the lesson. I stood fixed in the front of the classroom, unable to move, gripping the stick. I concentrated on not allowing my face to show my surprise. My heart raced.

I had bested Nakamura Sensei. In the eyes of the students, I had become the "Champion of the Kendo stick." From that day on, I held the stick from the start of class until the last student exited each time, my heart always pounding out of my chest.

Mine was only a small act of defiance. But I take pride in knowing that I spared those children a painful whack or two over the head for the remainder of my year in Japan. I wondered then – and continue to wonder today – why Nakamura Sensei didn't just hide the stick after I left class so that he would have unfettered access to it the next time we taught together. I guess it's too much trouble to hide a stick of that size. I like to think that I accomplished something that over a hundred years of Japanese law couldn't – I got through to Nakamura Sensei that violence has no place in the education process.

Interestingly, there have been no reported cases of corporal punishment in Japanese schools since 1995.

AMY ROSENBERG LOVES LANGUAGES. SHE HOLDS AN M.A. AND A B.A. IN LINGUISTICS AND SHE SPEAKS GERMAN, JAPANESE, AMERICAN SIGN LANGUAGE, SPANISH, AND ENGLISH. SHE LIVES ON THE EDGE OF THE WORLD IN HALF MOON BAY, CALIFORNIA, WHERE SHE USES HER LANGUAGE SKILLS TO WRITE CODE AND WRANGLE CHILDREN. IN 2007, SHE STARTED A FOOD BLOG CALLED SHE EATS! AMY CHRONICLES HER EXPERIENCES WITH FOOD AND LIFE AT AMYEATS.BLOGSPOT.COM. YOU CAN WATCH HER OLD COOKING VIDEOS ON YOUTUBE - YOUTUBE.COM/NEMICCOLOI.

35

Day Parents
By Dorrit Corwin

"If you can stomach his style, I might suggest a novel by Henry James," Dr. Long says, watching me scribble James's name at the end of a reading list that includes icons from Percy Shelley to Carmen Maria Machado. His ankles are crossed right over left, a mason jar in hand, as he thumbs through a pile of books he took off his shelf for me to consider. Dr. David Long prefers to be called "DL"; in his words, "The 'D' stands for 'Dave,' not 'Doctor.'" Dr. Banner, similarly nicknamed "DB," whips her silky gray bob around and audibly groans, "Oh Dave. You can't do that to her! Don't put her through the misery of reading Henry James."

Such is a typical lunch conversation in room C213. I burst in unannounced to swoon over Zadie Smith's essay on Joni Mitchell, and thirty minutes later I walk out with a stack of stellar reads. "Joni Mitchell, huh?" DL pauses for a moment. He clearly hasn't read her new collection of essays. He admits to it and does me one more:

"Why don't you pick out your two favorite essays from the anthology, and I'll have the class read and discuss them next week?" The gears in his brain are constantly turning. No syllabus is ever set in stone.

DL and DB are my day parents. They critique my work, praise my successes, and bicker with each other over their takes on feminist psychoanalysis and who to hire to fill in for teachers on maternity leave. Unlike with my real parents, I feel an inexplicable sense of exhilaration that stems from the simultaneous reverence and bewilderment that comes with being in their presence. I'm constantly searching for the right thing to say.

Like with most parent/child relationships, a long and winding road has led us to where we are. I spent my first four years at my all-girls private school frightened of the striking woman who was the co-head of the English department with the funny little man who was known to dress up as Hester Prynne during his teaching of *The Scarlet Letter*. In direct contrast to Dr. Long, Dr. Banner's aura was strict, critical, and intimidating. When she subbed one class for my ninth-grade English teacher, I could feel her judgment piercing the silence of fifteen frightened freshmen. But as I would later learn from her, it's all about word choice. Dr. Banner is rigorous, honest, and fierce. She exemplifies a tough love for the students in whom she identifies potential, which has altered the way I speak through writing just as much as it's changed the way I listen.

During the spring of tenth grade when I was selecting my junior year courses, I specifically requested not to have Dr. Banner for AP English. I did not want to be discouraged by a notoriously harsh teacher during the year of high school that mattered most. After my first year of English with Dr. Long, which was nothing short of a dream, I begged him to teach a section of AP English the following year. In fact, I wrote him a three-page "supplemental essay" confessing my love for his teaching style and seemingly endless knowledge, which ended with the sentence, "It's in your hands now..." As a man of critical theory and postmodern novellas, DL retired from the rigorous selection of British literature present in the

AP curriculum many years ago. I also now know that he secretly wanted to pass the baton of teaching me to Dr. Banner.

When I received my junior year schedule in the mail, I couldn't believe my eyes. I immediately emailed DL to inform him of my deep worries about having Dr. Banner as my teacher. His response was short and sweet: "I have an inkling you two are going to get along just swimmingly." To say his prediction proved accurate is an understatement.

In keeping with Freud's Oedipus complex, I've found myself so deeply enthralled with my day mom's eloquence and wisdom that my birth mother has developed deeply rooted feelings of inadequacy as a parent, who herself was an English major. When she met Dr. Banner, however, she completely understood where I was coming from. Debbie Banner captivates every room she walks into. People immediately stop what they're doing and, enveloped in her beauty and strong presence, listen to all she has to say. Her erudition, wit, and unparalleled expertise on everything from *Beowulf* to high school social situations is admirable and appreciated by all who know her.

Most notably, Dr. Banner embodies the core values and spirit of our tightly knit community. She is a fearless feminist who puts others before herself and holds herself and her students to impeccable standards. She transforms her students into inquisitive learners and conscientious people by teaching with precision, humor, and genuine care. I admitted to my friend and fellow "slut for the English department," as we call ourselves, that I simply must have a crush on Dr. Banner. There is no other way to describe the feeling I get every time I see her.

It has become a tradition that each year, a senior who had Dr. Banner her junior year will pass the million-dollar question on to a current junior: "Ask Dr. Banner to tell your class the story of her engagement." And she will. She will sacrifice an entire fifty-five-minute class period to regale her students with the beautiful story about meeting her husband as a freshman at Yale. Many of them cry, and not a single one forgets it.

I would most accurately compare Dr. Banner to a bottle of fine whiskey: classy, sophisticated, and audacious... strong, yet smooth. My real parents purchased a bottle for me to give to her as a parting gift at the end of our glorious year together. In her thank you note, she told me she would think of me every time she toasted to a glass, and she kindly extended an invitation to join her in an "intro to dark spirits" when I turn twenty-one.

This year, I'm back with Dr. Long, and better than ever. He has guided fifteen chosen future English majors through the complex origins of literary theory, all the way through contemporary applications from critical race theory to the neurohumanities. "This is a pretentious-safe space," DL told us on the first day of class. By the end of the year, we are each responsible for crafting a thirty page academic article on a topic of our choice. While I assumed the infamous "Senioritis" would've hit me like a truck by the springtime, I'm still wholeheartedly devoted to giving DL a good read. We miss Dr. Banner dearly, but I see her every time I pop my head into their shared classroom. She's always there to chat – about everything from books to college to boys.

After six years at my school, I've discovered what sets the legends apart. It isn't the PhD from Harvard or the resume peppered with prep schools that earn them the respect they deserve here. It's the teachers who understand what their students go through on a daily basis, the ones who teach their students the curriculum not through PowerPoint presentations and prepared activities, but through personal anecdotes that leave them with a feeling rather than pages of notes to memorize. It's the teachers who help their students improve by working with them, rather than against them. It's the ones who *care*—not only about the subjects they teach, but also about the girls to whom they teach. "It's not how widely you're loved, but rather, how deeply," I once told Dr. Long.

Parting with my day parents in May will be one of the most difficult transitions I've yet to overcome. But they've given me a second home like nothing I could've ever imagined. They've provided me with the tools to become not only the scholar I've always dreamed of being, but more importantly, a person of depth and empathy. As the late Michel Foucault once said, "I don't feel that it is necessary to know exactly what I am. The main interest in life and work is to become someone else that you were not in the beginning." Thank you both for taking me under your wings and transforming me into someone completely different than who I once was, in the best way possible.

DORRIT CORWIN IS CURRENTLY A SENIOR AT MARLBOROUGH SCHOOL IN LOS ANGELES WHERE SHE SERVES AS EDITOR-IN-CHIEF OF THE ART-AND-LITERATURE MAGAZINE AND WRITES A MUSIC COLUMN FOR THE SCHOOL NEWSPAPER. SHE IS THE RECIPIENT OF TWO SCHOLASTIC GOLD KEYS, ONE FOR A SHORT STORY SHE WROTE AT THE KENYON REVIEW YOUNG WRITERS' WORKSHOP, AND ONE FOR AN ESSAY SHE WROTE ABOUT THE COLLEGE BOARD MONOPOLY. DORRIT IS A GRADUATE OF THE RISING VOICES FELLOWSHIP, A MEMBER OF THE EDITORIAL BOARD AT FRESH INK FOR TEENS, AND AN ASPIRING SCREENWRITER. DORRIT WILL BE ATTENDING BROWN UNIVERSITY IN THE FALL. FIND DORRIT ATWWW.DORRITCORWIN.COM.

36

My Teachers Didn't Just Teach Me Academics; They Taught Me
Valuable Life Lessons
By Katie Bingham-Smith

I had a horrible stuttering problem when I was young. My father would sit with me and remind me to slow down, to speak clearly, to stop and think before I began a sentence. I was only about four when this started to creep into my life, but I remember very clearly his face close to mine, looking at his dark beard holding in bursts of laughter because he looked so serious and I could see up his nose.

I'd get so excited to talk, I needed to get those thoughts that were racing in my head out as if they were on fire. My problem was I tried to spit them out as fast as they were racing through my mind and the result would make me get stuck on my "Ss" or "Ms." The harder I tried to pronounce something, the more it got stuck in the back of my throat, only allowing one sound to come out over and over and over until I'd give up.

This faded a bit as I got older but would creep up from time to time if I got nervous. Nothing made my stuttering flare like having to read out loud in front of the class. I hated doing anything that required me to stand up in front of my peers unless I felt I was good at it. And for a long time, I wasn't a good reader.

When I was in second grade, I changed schools, moving from California to Maine in the middle of December. I remember feeling gloomy and sad. The days were so short and the sky was so gray, and why did everyone wear ugly duck boots on their feet? I missed my flip-flops and fluorescent green sunglasses.

But most of all, I missed the group of friends I'd had in California. I went to a bilingual school and we'd talk to each other in Spanish at recess on the monkey bars after eating bologna sandwiches and trading bags of chips. My teacher was sweet, and she never made anyone read out loud in front of the whole class. Instead, we'd break up in small groups, take turns reading, and she would come visit our little pods and listen. She'd always put her hand on my shoulder if I began to stutter, and just like that, the blockage would clear and the words would come.

Sitting in my new classroom in Maine during my first week there, my teacher started the morning by having us take turns reading aloud. I looked down at the book we were reading; the text was big with lots of pictures and I knew all the words, yet my heart was pounding as it got closer to my turn and I felt my hot cheeks with my cool hand. This was coming easy to all the other kids; no one else felt nervous, and so I had no doubt I'd be fine since they were.

As she called my name, I was able to read the first sentence and then I froze. I'm still not sure if I was stuck on the word "surprise" or if my confidence plummeted because I said "of" instead of "if" as the story was written, and I heard snickering from the back of the class.

I looked to my teacher for support; maybe she'd put her hand on my shoulder, or tell me to take my time, or get me started by saying, "surp..." I knew what the word was, but it wasn't coming and I began to panic.

My teacher didn't walk toward me and touch my shoulder; she

didn't tell me to take my time. Instead, she asked me if I was retarded in front of the whole class as I struggled to pronounce the word—in front of these new kids I didn't quite know yet but wanted so desperately to fit in with.

After that, I fell in love with reading. I decided I'd be damned if something like that was ever going to happen to me again (it never did), but I learned something from that experience: I was a good reader, I was not a quitter, and I could be called every name in the book after that day because there was something in our exchange that made resilient, and wanting to prove her wrong. She lit a fire under my ass and forced me to explore and tackle reading and writing in a way I wouldn't have otherwise.

Throughout my schooling I was met over and over by teachers who lifted me up when I was struggling—not just with a word while reading aloud, but with their raw support.

Like my fourth-grade teacher who all the kids called "mean and strict." She held me to a standard she knew I was capable of. Also, she had the best pair of purple corduroy pants I coveted. "I love your pants," I told her one day while she was checking in on my social studies report progress. "If you get an A on this report, you can have them when you grow into them," she said. That never happened, but man did I work my ass off of that report with visions of myself sporting those pants with a side ponytail. She knew how to motivate me.

And my fifth-grade teacher who knew I was struggling with a group of girls and took the time to check in on me, call my mother to let her know what was going on after she'd worked a long day, and went home to her two kids. That year, math was difficult for me partly because of the girl drama, but also because I was beginning to hate math. All I wanted to do was read chapter books and write poems and short stories. My father told me if I got a B in math that year, he'd buy me a new bike. Not only did she know about this deal my father had made with me, she told the whole class on the last day of school after she watched me open my report card and whisper "Yes!" as I looked at that stunning B-plus. She was jumping and cheering and got everyone so excited. I wasn't the only student she celebrated victories with. She was exceptional.

My sixth-grade teacher let a group and friends and me take time out of the classroom to write a play. Then, he gave us permission to put on a performance in front of the whole school. We were pretty sure we were all going to be Broadway stars after that, but alas, we weren't. He made us feel like we would be though.

In tenth grade when I was struggling with an eating disorder, it was my English teacher who pulled me aside and wanted to talk about it. She told me she was here for me and let me know she felt it was severe enough to tell the school nurse, who called my parents. She jump-started my road to recovery by taking ten minutes out of her busy day to talk to me.

None of these teachers who touched my life in immeasurable ways had to do these things, but they did. They changed my life; they supported me in ways that weren't always academic-based. And when I think about it now, I am in awe.

They all had families of their own to worry about. They were putting in a lot of extra time they weren't getting paid for, they had a lasting impression on me that has stuck in my soul over the years—even my second-grade teacher.

I thought of her when I was applying for a scholarship after getting accepted to my school of choice and deciding to major in English with a concentration in creative writing—a scholarship I was awarded.

I thought of her when I got my first piece accepted to *Architectural Digest*, and the first time I was published in a book. I think of her every time I pick something to read, when I read out loud to my kids, or when open my laptop to write.

I also think of all the other teachers who put time and effort into me; time and effort they may not have always been able to afford or invest in, but they did. And because they decided to do that instead of tending to their mountains of paperwork, or go talk to the other teachers in the lounge, or decide they had done enough and were just too tired, I was taught I was worth investing in, that I mattered, that school wasn't just about getting good grades.

They taught me how to treat people and how to treat myself—that can't be taught from a textbook. And at forty-three, I can say they were the ones who taught me the most important life lessons.

KATIE BINGHAM-SMITH HAD THREE KIDS IN THREE YEARS AND CRAFTS HER ASS OFF IN ORDER TO STAY SANE. SHE LOVES TO WRITE, WEAR FAUX LEATHER PANTS, EAT AT BURGER JOINTS, AND MAKE BEAUTIFUL THINGS. SHE PAYS HER KIDS TO RUB HER FEET AND PLAY WITH HER HAIR. YOU CAN SEE MORE ON INSTAGRAM @KATIEBINGHAMSMITH.

37

You Teach What?!?!
By Amy Bozza

I have taught in a middle school for the past twenty-three years. When I'm at some type of social gathering and people ask what I do, their response is either, "Oh wow! You are so lucky! I love middle schoolers!" or, more commonly, "Middle school? Are you crazy? You couldn't pay me enough to teach middle school."

Ironically, there seems to be no middle ground with middle school.

Yet, that is the unique beauty of teaching the middle grades. Every single day you walk into school expecting one thing and wind up with something completely different.

Chalk it up to hormones. Chalk it up to growing pains. Chalk it up to whatever you want.

At the end of the day, the cause doesn't matter. Middle school is a beautiful crapshoot.

Let's be honest ...

Teaching any grade is awesome and yet full of challenges.

I'd love to teach elementary school because it would be lovely to teach students that still think their teacher is the sun and the moon and the stars.

But with four children of my own, I have enough noses to wipe and shoes to tie, and there are only so many topics that you can discuss with elementary students, as so many things that are happening in the world are too big for small children to comprehend, analyze, or deal with.

As a teacher of social studies, teaching high school would be amazing as well because of the depth we could get into regarding certain topics. In addition, the students would have had many more years of in-depth historical study under their belts to provide stronger background knowledge as we looked for patterns in societal behavior.

Yet, in high school, the stakes are higher, which ramps up the anxieties in the students (and the parents) and everyone is focused on the grade, the GPA, the class rank, and learning for learning's sake begins to disappear.

Middle school is the sweet spot. Eighth-grade, the sweetest of all.

Eighth-graders are beginning to think for themselves but want to know what we think. Still like us enough to want to connect with us on a personal level, but are too cool to tell us. They walk around the building like they own the place, yet write journal entries about how they are terrified that people will find out that they definitely don't have it all figured out.

And the best part is that there are experiences you can have as a middle school teacher that most likely wouldn't happen anywhere else because of who eighth-graders are.

For example, let's talk about the eighth-grade trip.

The pinnacle of the eighth-grade year, at our school, is the eighth grade trip to Washington, DC. and I have the good fortune of organizing, coordinating, and running the trip.

And I do not use the term "good fortune" sarcastically. It is a pleasure and an honor to offer this trip to these students.

With approximately 350 eighth-graders each year, our trip lasts two days and one night. Only teachers chaperone the trip, and parents are not allowed.

And while people think I'm crazy for teaching middle school, when they hear that I run a trip that takes 350 eighth-graders out of state, overnight, they think I'm absolutely certifiable.

Our district is extremely diverse in every sense of the word. We have students from many countries, who speak a variety of languages, who practice myriad religions, with every color of skin. We also have students who are living in homeless shelters sitting in classes next to students who are living in million-dollar homes.

Our school is a proud microcosm of American society and we love it.

Throughout the year, I run fundraisers, fairly consistently, in order to make sure all of our students can enjoy the trip...not just the students who can pay for it. And the students who need the help are often the ones who have never, and will never, leave New Jersey, much less our town, ever again.

These students consistently thank us, over and over again, for providing them with this opportunity, and so, again I say, it is a pleasure and an honor to run this trip.

While running the DC trip, I have learned a little something each year. It didn't always run smoothly. The trip today is completely different from the trip I ran the first year. I've modified, changed, added, and deleted based on what went wrong and what went right on each journey. But the kids? The kids always roll with whatever the trip throws at them every single time. Because that's eighth grade.

In the first year of the DC trip, we realized what a large group we had and decided to go with a tour company that was offering a very low rate for travel.

Upon checking into the hotel we began to panic.

The doors to each room opened to a parking lot, as there were no inner hallways to keep the students contained. There were strange stains on the walls, and when the students began to shower, we realized there was also no hot water in the entire building.

And yet, there was laughter. So much laughter that year.

One of our teachers, who was particularly tough in class and as a result was not necessarily a student favorite, was checking in on four of her students and found them huddled on one bed due to a roach in the corner of their room.

She killed the roach, checked under every bed, went through every nook and cranny of the room, and then took the girls back to her room (after calling each of their parents for permission), where they slept in her beds and she slept in a chair, because they were still afraid that more roaches would appear while they slept.

For the rest of the year, that teacher was their hero and entered any room to thunderous applause.

We went to each room to explain to the students how to take a "Hokey-Pokey" shower.

You put your one arm in, you put your one arm out, you put your one leg in, you put your one leg out, because no one could possibly submerge their entire body in the freezing cold water that was pouring out of the shower head.

As we passed their doors, we could hear the students screaming with laughter as they executed their Hokey-Pokey showers, and the students who were able to stand the temps the longest boasted, as if it were a badge of honor.

In the morning, the students offered to buy coffee for the teachers who forewent sleep to stand in the parking lot and watch all of the doors to make sure the students didn't try to leave their rooms, but also to make sure no one tried to get in. I spent more time in the management office that year than I have ever spent in a management office *anywhere*, and we were only at the hotel for ten hours.

It was a mess. A hot mess.

Yet, every year, we have students who traveled with us that year reach out and say "Hey, it's May and a few of us were just talking about that awesome trip to DC we took with you guys! Remember the Roach Motel? It was the most fun we had ever had!"

Because, if you remember eighth-grade, everything is a disaster; everything is chaos. And when you live in chaos, you learn to find the fun in the little things, even when it seems like things are falling apart.

Each year, we check their luggage, because we would be crazy not to, but in middle school, it's not drugs or alcohol we find.

When we open up the luggage, we pull things like aromatherapy candles with matches out of the suitcases of girls who want to have a "spa night" in their hotel room. Or a bag of homemade slime from a backpack of a kid who thought it would be fun to play with in case he got bored.

And then there was the year that we found three feet of heavy metal chain. When I asked the young man why he was bringing the chain, the response was, "Just in case, Mrs. Bozza. Just in case."

One year, our tour guide popped open her Confederate flag umbrella in front of our diverse student body and then, when I immediately approached her about it, she had no understanding of why our students were offended.

When I returned to the group, the students came to me and said, "Thanks for trying. It's okay. Some people just don't know any better."

And then there was the year when we received an automated call from the district that there were verified cases of the H1N1 virus back at school. Students' cell phones started ringing with the news that siblings were infected, and immediately the kids started asking for masks so they wouldn't expose the rest of us to the virus. They were terrified they were sick, but their first concern was that they didn't make the rest of us ill as well.

Another year, we traveled to DC and the air conditioning on our bus died.

It very quickly began to resemble a rainforest on our bus. A rainforest full of hormonal children whose sweat glands were working overtime to produce the most malodorous fumes.

When the air broke, the windshield began to sweat, as well, and the chaperones on the bus began to take turns standing next to the bus driver, wiping the large pane of glass clear.

One by one, we would take fifteen minute shifts, until our arms started to burn and the perspiration began to sting our eyes, and then we would tag in the next chaperone to take the towel and become the internal windshield wiper.

The students embraced the situation and began to cheer us on, singing songs for us, and generally calling out, "You got this, guys!" or "You can do it!"

And we did. For four hours.

We've had buses break down, hit cars, and even catch fire (not while the students were on the bus), all to the gleeful delight of the children. To them, it's a grand adventure.

They even embraced the year that our bus driver decided to go rogue. He knew *all* the shortcuts. For those two days, it felt like we never got off the bus, as every "shortcut" he knew landed us in at least 40 minutes of extra heavy downtown DC traffic.

The kids on our bus missed at least three of the things we were supposed to see and the other seven buses wound up waiting for us, at the last rest stop before home, for an hour and a half before our driver finally rolled in.

But our kids cheered and sang and thanked the bus driver every time they got on and off that bus.

The truth is, the eighth-graders wouldn't care if we never got off the bus in DC. They love the ride.

On my bus, we play games with the kids, and because they are eighth graders, they play. They wrestle with the fact that they want to play because it's not cool, but they are tempted by the possibility for fun, and eventually, even we are surprised by the kids who play our games.

Students who have uttered nary a word in class all year will suddenly sing commercial jingles and TV show theme songs in our "Bus Idol" competition. They celebrate the cheesy Dollar Store prizes we stock up on before the trip, and boys and girls alike will wear the goggles, the tiaras, the fake eyelashes, or the dollar sign on a fake gold chain, that they won on the bus, to school for the rest of the year.

They joke with the tour guide, but they pay close enough attention that their hands are shooting up in the air during the trivia competitions on the way home.

They revel in "Chaperone Trivia" where they try to guess things about our lives and desperately try not to hurt our feelings as they answer questions like "Put the chaperones in order from oldest to youngest," and beg us to share the stories behind the answers to the question "Which of your teachers served a detention when they were in middle school?"

They dance and sing and ask us to join them on the dance floor during the dinner cruise, where we hold the eighth-grade dance, because we still exist for them. We are not invisible adults who are just there to keep them in line. They want us there and they want to bond with us in the ways that they know how.

And as rowdy and loud and joyful and goofy as they are on the bus, they stand in absolute, respectful silence for thirty minutes at the Tomb of the Unknown Soldier while they wait for the changing of the guard, and they thank and shake hands with veterans at the Vietnam Memorial.

You see, it is *because* eighth-graders are different people every single day that they are so flexible and when something is expected of them, they know who to be at just the right moment.

Two years ago, our bus driver couldn't find a parking space in front of our usual departure point, and when he texted me to tell me where he was, his location was three blocks away from where the other four chaperones, fifty students, and I were waiting on our bus.

So, we began to walk, and suddenly, the skies went dark, the clouds opened up, and we were caught in a deluge the likes of which I had never seen before and haven't seen since. We began to run with the kids, laughing and dancing and singing like lunatics. Kids from all walks of life, together, enjoying the moment, making the memory.

When we boarded the bus, we all appeared to have jumped in a pool, fully clothed, and we sat in those wet clothes for the next six hours.

Not one of those fifty students complained.

Not. One.

But perhaps the best example I could give of the beauty of eighth graders is that I give my cell phone number to 350 eighth-graders every single year, on the DC trip. I give it to them in case of emergency, so that there is one adult contact they know is on-call no matter the time of day or night while we are on that trip.

In all the years I've given them my number, not one of them has ever used that number for anything other than an emergency.

(That I know of.)

Because eighth-graders are awesome.

I use the DC trip to demonstrate their unique and wonderful personalities because it is the one time of the year that we are all together, but each of us who teach in a middle school can share a million stories that happen right in our classrooms as well.

If you ask any adult what school year they would never want to repeat, the majority will tell you that there isn't enough money in the world to make them want to relive middle school.

Middle schoolers are complicated.

They are happy at noon and in tears by one. They are enemies in November and best friends in January. They are 5'6" in September and 5'9" by April.

But they are ours, and damn, we love these little people.

And when June rolls around, they leave us. We stand with them at graduation and we say goodbye as they march out of the door. And it hurts.

It hurts because we aren't just spectators of their lives. We actually walk with them on the journey, from who they once were to the new people they have become. We've cried with them and laughed with them and we have been their greatest fans.

So, call me crazy if you want, but I say I'm lucky that I get to spend every day with these complicated, confused, amazing humans, and I wouldn't want it any other way.

AMY BOZZA IS AN EIGHTH-GRADE HISTORY TEACHER IN NEW JERSEY AND HAS BEEN AN EDUCATOR FOR APPROXIMATELY TWENTY-FIVE YEARS, GIVE OR TAKE A FEW MATERNITY LEAVES. WHEN SHE ISN'T BUSY TEACHING YOUR KIDS, SHE'S TEACHING PIANO TO OTHER PEOPLE'S KIDS,

OR HOME HANGING OUT WITH HER HUSBAND AND THEIR FOUR KIDS. AMY IS A CONTRIBUTOR TO THE BESTSELLING *I JUST WANT TO PEE ALONE* ANTHOLOGY AND HAS HAD AN ESSAY ABOUT TEACHING PUBLISHED IN THE HUFFINGTON POST. SINCE HER YOUNGEST CHILD IS ONLY SEVEN, SHE FIGURES TO GET HIM THROUGH COLLEGE SHE'LL BE TEACHING UNTIL THEY HAVE TO ROLL HER OUT OF THE BUILDING IN A BODY BAG. BUT THAT'S OKAY BECAUSE SHE TRULY DOES LOVE HER JOB.

38

Lessons Without a Test
By Julie Burton

I don't consider myself a smart person.

Don't throw the book to the ground—keep reading. Isn't that what teachers taught us?

Read.

I still use calculators to figure out a tip. I get lost everywhere I go because I believe the North Star points up, not north. I was *shocked* when I found out Ricky Martin is gay. I thank police officers for speeding tickets. I sit, stare, and blink at my kid's long division homework because my brain pulls up the color black.

It's been fifteen years since I listened to a teacher's lecture, but that doesn't mean I haven't stopped learning. Google is a good teacher in a pinch. I am at an age where I ask questions without embarrassment if I don't understand something. I am a CIA-level spy when it comes to keeping track of my older kids with cell phones.

The kids.

My kids shake up memories.

The memories float to the surface. It's like someone jumping feet first into the shallow ocean or lake and touching the bottom. The debris floats up. *Don't gag. It's a metaphor.* No one told me I would relive my childhood when I became a parent. I'm growing up again, but I'm on the other side of the camera lens.

Every time my kids start a new grade, my feet hit the bottom of the ocean and my own teachers float up. Nearly twenty years of memories flood back into focus. I didn't know it at the time, but my teachers taught me lessons they never tested me on.

"Look me in the eyes. You love yourself, okay?"
      Ms. Funk, seventh-grade, Physical Education

"OH MY GOD, YOUR BACK!" the girl next to my gym locker yelled. I yanked my PE shirt over my head. "YOU HAVE BLOOD ON YOUR BACK!" A few other girls turned and looked at me. I looked down at my hands and shut my locker.

"Oh, I don't know," I said. I didn't know what else to say.

The girl next to me whispered, "You are SO WEIRD. You're sitting too close to me. Scoot over."

I scooted. The glass window shook next to my PE locker. *Why is my locker next to the teacher's office? Why can't my locker be hiding in the corner?* Ms. Funk pointed at me and pointed to her desk. Another teacher walked out to take my class roll call.

"Hi, Ms. Funk," I said.

"Julie, what's going on? What happened?" Ms. Funk inquired.

Middle school PE teachers intimidated me. I didn't have a real reason other than I didn't like their rules. We had to announce when we were on our periods during roll call. *Partial* was the code word. Middle school PE was the first time I changed clothes in front of strangers. Showers were required after swim days and no swimsuits were allowed. The showers were open with no privacy. Middle school PE teachers had the job of telling a room full of thirteen-year-old girls to get naked in front their peers, at least on swim days. I was terrified of them.

"I...um, well this boy has been bothering me a little bit. In science class," I said. A strange guilt rushed through me. Ms. Funk asked to see my back. I turned around and let her lift my shirt. I felt a tug where the blood dried.

"JESUS. WHAT IS THIS?" she gasped. Ms. Funk pulled a tissue from her desk. She dabbed at the bloodstains.

"Well, this boy took an X-Acto knife and stabbed me in the back. He sits behind me," I said.

"This is more than one stab," Ms. Funk responded. "How long has this been going on?" She pulled my shirt back down over my back and tapped my shoulder. I turned around. I dropped my head and lowered my voice, "I mean, I told him to stop, but he doesn't listen. It's my fault. I should have said something to the teacher, but I don't want him to be angry if I tell."

"This is assault. I'm notifying the parents and the administration. Julie, this will never happen again. You don't need to worry about retaliation, I promise you. You're not in trouble, and this is not your fault. You think this is your fault? Look me in the eyes," she said. I looked up at her. She looked shocked but her eyes told me she was heartbroken. "You love yourself, okay?"

I nodded, "Okay."

The boy never spoke to me again. His family moved away the next year. In middle school PE, the only lesson I learned was from Ms. Funk. I remembered to love myself.

"Rules never make a good show."
Mrs. Hungerford, twelfth-grade, Fashion

Taking fashion in high school meant you would be in charge of the spring and fall fashion shows. The productions brought a sold-out auditorium filled with teachers, administration, parents, and students. The models were the fashion students. The clothes were on loan from local boutiques. There was a high level of commitment when you signed up for Mrs. H's fashion class.

Her name is Mrs. H. because Mrs. Hungerford made it clear that the real Mrs. Hungerford is her mother-in-law and she can never be called that.

I volunteered to lead the set design. "You guys, for swimwear, I have an idea," I said as I drew a quick drawing of the stage, "My dad owns a boat company. I wonder if we can pull a boat on the stage and have the models stand on it before they come down the runway."

"BRILLIANT!" Mrs. H yelled as she overheard my plans.

I laughed. Another idea sparked. "And for the heavy metal scene, my dad and Uncle Bruce have Harleys. If we can haul a boat, why not have them ride a few motorcycles in before the scene? They can sit on each side of the runway. "Julie, this is amazing," a classmate said, "and this is less work for us."

Dress rehearsal arrived. My dad hauled the boat to the docking doors and the school staff helped guide the boat to the stage. My dad asked Mrs. H where to ride the Harleys.

"ABSOLUTELY NOT," said the theater teacher. "We can't have them riding Harleys on the stage. We won't be held responsible if there's an accident. And with those the fumes running? NO." Mrs. H laughed and said, "We'll kill the Harleys once they're parked." The theater teacher said he would get the principal involved if he had to. I suggested my dad and uncle push the Harleys on stage in between scenes and sit on them.

It was opening night of the fashion show. The curtain lifted and the audience "oooo'ed" at the boat filled with models. The first scene was over. I changed backstage as my dad and the school staff pulled the boat off. Another scene began and ended. The next scene was heavy metal. I ran to the side of the stage to make sure the Harleys got pushed on.

The lights went out. It was pitch black. The audience fell quiet. This wasn't in the plan. My friends and I tried to find each other with our hands. We couldn't see anything. Murmurs came from the audience. I wondered if we lost power.

Harleys roared to life and two headlights showed up on the side of the stage. My mouth dropped as I covered my eyes from the blinding headlights. The motorcycles revved up. They revved again, louder. "HELLS ANGELS!" someone screamed from the audience. My dad and Uncle Bruce did a circle on the stage. The motorcycles echoed so loud the building shook. Gasoline fumes filled the auditorium. They parked the Harleys where they were told and killed the motors. Like magic, the stage lights turned on and two men dressed in leather sat cross-armed on Harley-Davidsons. The scene began with a standing ovation.

I found Mrs. H backstage. She was clapping and had tears in her eyes. She looked at me and said, "Rules never make a good show. What are they going to do? Fire me?"

Mrs. H never got in trouble by the school. If she did, I never heard about it. If you're going to break the rules, you better have Hells Angels behind your back.

"I think I'm going to go hiking in the Rocky Mountains this weekend. Yeah. It's decided."
    Dr. Gould, College level, Advertising

"Dr. Tom Gould passed away on Sunday, February 14, 2016 at his home after a long battle against cancer."

I stared at the screen. It was 2018.

My daughter asked me what college is like. I opened my computer to show her my favorite professor.

I swallowed hard and closed my eyes.

It was 2003 and I was packing my pens and notebooks in my backpack. I was getting ready to leave Gould's advertising class. The difference between teachers and professors is professors don't give a shit. Show up for class. Get straight As. Skip class. Show up to class drunk. Professors do not care about your life choices. Gould took *not a giving a shit* to a new level.

"You know what? I'm going to go hiking in the Rocky Mountains this weekend. Yeah. It's decided," Gould announced to the class. It sounded like a random thought, yet we knew he had every intention of carrying it through.

Gould taught class in the moment with a sort of assertive mindfulness that's talked about today but not in 2004. He spoke his thoughts out loud for anyone to hear. Many of his classes were taught as an open discussion. One class assignment was to bring any quote from any book and read it to the class. We discussed why the words we picked touched us in some way. We saw Gould as a friend rather than a professor.

I looked over at my classmate Nick. "He's so funny! Going to Colorado this weekend?! Okay, done." I laughed.

Nick said, "You know why Gould lives in the moment, don't you? He's a brain cancer survivor. He lives his life how he wants. He took a group of students out for beers once just because he felt like it. He's cool. You should come with us next time!"

The memory faded. Tears filled my eyes.

His spirit arrived in my present moment. I guess you could say his spirit has always been in my present moments, at least for the past fifteen years. I never got to say a proper goodbye. Dr. Tom Gould, a professor at the highest level of education, left me one lesson—go outside, have a beer, and live your life.

This essay is dedicated to you, Gould.

JULIE BURTON IS A MOM, WIFE, HUMOR WRITER, AND BACON-HATER LIVING IN OVERLAND PARK, KANSAS. SHE IS A CONTRIBUTING WRITER AND COLUMNIST IN SIMPLYKC MAGAZINE. SHE IS ALSO A REGULAR CONTRIBUTING WRITER IN FILTER FREE PARENTS. BURTON IS A CONTRIBUTING AUTHOR TO TWO ANTHOLOGIES: BUT DID YOU DIE?: SETTING THE PARENTING BAR LOW AND THE UNOFFICIAL GUIDE TO SURVIVING PREGNANCY WITHOUT LOSING YOUR MIND. HER WORK HAS APPEARED IN THE GOOD MEN PROJECT, SAMMICHES AND PSYCH MEDS, MOCK MOMS, AND MY LIFE SUCKERS. SHE IS CONSISTENTLY NAMED ONE OF THE FUNNIEST PARENTS ON THE HUFFINGTON POST.

AND YES, SHE REALLY DOES HATE BACON. PLEASE DON'T DROP HER AS A FRIEND.

39

How Moving to Kansas, a Couple of Off-Duty Teachers, and Lucy van
Pelt Helped Me Find My Superpower
By Jen Mann

W hen I was sixteen, my parents moved me from New
Jersey to Kansas. It was like moving to another planet
as far as I was concerned. I didn't expect to stay long,
though. They'd tried to move me to the Midwest before and failed.
When I was in seventh grade, they moved me to Illinois. I went to
school there for less than a week. I remember nothing about that
school except my locker combination and the library, which is where
I hid out when I skipped every class.

After three days of sobbing to my parents, we moved back to New
Jersey just in time to start school again. I have two first-day-of-school
pictures from that year. My tiny sixteen-year-old brain thought we
moved away from Illinois because I cried and threw a temper
tantrum. My tiny sixteen-year-old brain thought my happiness was so
important to my parents that they moved me back to New Jersey.

So, once we got settled into the new house in Kansas, I told my friends, "I'll be back in a week, save my seat at lunch." And then I threw a fit and demanded to go back to New Jersey.

But my parents were like, "Yeah, when we left Illinois a few years ago, it wasn't because of you, dummy. Dad got a better job offer back in Jersey, so we moved. That's not happening again, because this is where Grandma lives and we're never leaving."

NOOOOOOOOOOOOOOOOOOOO!

I couldn't believe it. I was shocked. It was as if my feelings didn't matter at all.

My brother was in sixth grade and he did much better with the transition. In sixth grade, teachers still made you feel welcome and asked other kids to sit by you. First day of my sophomore year, I was handed a schedule and a map of the school and told, "Good luck."

I made exactly zero friends.

Right away my parents found a church to attend. Church had always been a big part of my life growing up. In New Jersey our church was very small and we'd never had a youth group. My mom made a huge deal that they picked this particular church because there was a very large and active group of high school students who met every Wednesday night for Bible study or something.

Greeeeat, I thought. *Just what I need. A bunch of holy rollers.*

At our first youth group meeting I found out we didn't do Bible study. It was actually pizza and a lot of volleyball and maybe a prayer at the end. So much better than I'd anticipated, but still, lame. The kids kind of ignored me, so I was introduced to all of the adult leaders. I mostly muttered, "'Sup?" and picked at my cuticles, but one in particular seemed to take an interest in me.

Calvin was a burly, hairy, sweaty guy with a giant mustache. He asked me to get up in front of the group and introduce myself.

Thirty years later, I am happy to jump on any stage and entertain a crowd of friends, family, or strangers, but back then "wallflower" would have been too strong of a word to use to describe me. I wanted to die.

"I can't," I whispered.

Calvin's wife, Dora, sidled up. "Hi," she said, smiling. "How's it going?"

"I think Jenni should introduce herself to the group. Tell us where she's from, where she goes to high school, what she does in her free time, that sort of thing," Calvin said.

"Good idea," Dora agreed.

Ugh. I wanted to yell, *I'm Jenni. I'm from Jersey. Don't get attached, because I'm going back ASAP. I go to the dumbest high school in this town with the most stuck-up snobs and my free time is spent imagining them all in comas!* But because normal people don't say stuff like that out loud, I said, "Terrible idea."

Dora nodded, but Calvin was a pusher. "How come?" he asked.

When I am uncomfortable and feel backed into a corner, I cannot be honest or vulnerable about my feelings. Instead I lash out. I'm like a defensive little chipmunk. "Because this is so stupid! There's no sense getting to know anyone here! They're all weird."

"And you're not weird?" Calvin asked, his mustache twitching.

"Of course not!" I said, baring my teeth.

"Come on, when you think about it, isn't everyone a little weird, Jenni?" Calvin asked.

"No, I think just you are," I snapped.

Calvin turned to the crowd and clapped his hands to silence the rowdy teenagers. Once it was quiet he announced, "Hey, everybody! This is Jenni and she's..." I waited for him say "weird" but instead he said, "funny. Her sense of humor is a little dark, but I think if you give her a chance, you'll really like her. Let's all make Jenni feel welcome, okay?"

After that kids came over and greeted me. He'd broken the ice for me.

Over the next several weeks I grew quite close to Calvin and his wife, Dora. I found out Calvin was a high school guidance counselor (not at my school, unfortunately) and Dora was a music teacher. Even though they both spent all week dealing with other people's teenagers, they gave up their Wednesday nights to hang out with even more teenagers! It was a good thing, though, because they both had a gift when it came to dealing with prickly teenagers like me.

There were days I didn't want to get out of bed and go to school, but my parents would threaten to take away my Wednesday night youth group meeting. Just knowing that Calvin and Dora would be waiting for me on a Wednesday night with a strong embrace and a sympathetic-but-also-a-healthy-dose-of-tough-love speech would motivate me.

We were always doing fundraisers to pay for mission trips or camps or whatever and one night Dora announced we were going to try something different from our usual wrapping paper and cookie dough sales. "We're going to host a dinner theater and sell tickets!"

"What is that?" I asked.

"It's just what it sounds like: ticket holders get dinner and a show," Calvin said.

"But who's doing the show?" someone asked.

"You kids are doing the show," Dora said. "You're going to put on a musical. And Jenni's dad has offered to cook the meal."

I groaned. *Of course he did,* I thought. I smelled a rat. This was a bunch of adults conspiring against me to try and get me involved in shit, but I wasn't going to fall for it. I had no musical talent. I had terrible stage fright. There was no way I was even auditioning for this play!

"We're doing *You're a Good Man, Charlie Brown,* and Dora and I have already assigned you parts," Calvin said. He pulled out a piece of paper and started reading aloud. I stared at my Doc Martens and wondered if I could fake the flu or something and go home early. "...and Jenni Mann will be Lucy van Pelt."

My head snapped up. What? Lucy van Pelt? The girl who always pulls the football away before Charlie Brown can kick it? The lunatic? That's the part they gave me? Clearly I misread my relationship with Dora and Calvin. We weren't friends. They thought I was a bitch! I felt tears well up in my eyes and I looked for an exit. I did not want anyone to see me crying.

I made a beeline for the door and headed out into the parking lot, fumbling for my car keys. I heard the door open behind me and I heard Dora call my name.

Calvin caught up to me first with Dora fast on his heels. "What's going on, Jenni?" Calvin asked.

I couldn't hold the tears back any longer. I wailed, "You think I'm a bully! You made me the worst character in the whole play!"

Dora looked stricken. "No!" she exclaimed, reaching for me. "No, not at all!"

"Yes! She's awful. She's the worst. Everyone hates Lucy! Why would you make me Lucy?"

Calvin shook his head. "You don't get it, do you?" he asked.

"Get what?" I demanded.

"Lucy is the star. Lucy has the best lines in the whole show. Lucy is hilarious. Yes, she's gruff, but she knows who she is and she's not ashamed of herself. She likes herself and she doesn't care what anyone thinks of her. You can be Lucy, but you're too worried about what everyone thinks of you."

"I do not!"

"You're out here crying in a parking lot because you think we don't like you," Dora said, gently.

I snorted. "Okay, yeah, maybe I care a little bit."

Dora hugged me. "You care a lot," she whispered, releasing me.

Calvin grasped my shoulders and looked me square in the eyes, "You are hilarious, Jenni Mann, but no one knows that. Dora and I talk about you all week and look forward to laughing at the stories you tell us every Wednesday night. The other people around here just think you're quiet, but we know the real you, and we're going to help you show everyone who you are. You're going to get on that stage and you're going to show everyone how funny you are. You're going to *become* Lucy van Pelt, and you're going to steal that show. I guarantee it."

～

A FEW MONTHS later I stood on the stage, raised my fist, and uttered Lucy's immortal words, *"These five fingers...individually they're nothing, but when I curl them together like this into a single unit, they form a weapon that is terrible to behold!"*

The room erupted in laughter and I paused a beat like Dora had taught me, waiting for the laughter to die down before I continued threatening poor Linus, and let the feeling of euphoria wash over me. Calvin was right. I became Lucy that night. I tried to steal some of Lucy's confidence and swagger, and I tried to let go of the anger and frustration I'd been feeling for months. Yes, Lucy's a bitch, but as my BFF Tina Fey would say years later, "Bitches get stuff done."

There was no way that when Calvin and Dora gave sixteen-year-old me that line none of us would know that I'd grow up to write humor books called *People I Want to Punch in the Throat*. All they knew was I was a misfit kid looking for my place in the world and they could see that humor could maybe be my thing, but I needed more confidence in myself. They gave me a taste of what it felt like to make a roomful of people laugh, and they helped me see that that's a motherfucking superpower.

Calvin and Dora were an integral part to helping me find my voice, and I will forever be grateful to both of them for sticking with a sullen, miserable, sarcastic teenager who was stuck in Kansas against her will.

Not to be dramatic, but I'm pretty sure those two (and Lucy van Pelt), like, totally saved my life!

JEN MANN IS BEST KNOWN FOR HER WILDLY POPULAR AND HYSTERICAL BLOG PEOPLE I WANT TO PUNCH IN THE THROAT. SHE HAS BEEN DESCRIBED BY MANY AS ERMA BOMBECK' WITH F-BOMBS. JEN IS KNOWN FOR HER HILARIOUS RANTS AND FUNNY OBSERVATIONS. JEN IS THE AUTHOR OF THE *NEW YORK TIMES* BESTSELLER *PEOPLE I WANT TO PUNCH IN THE THROAT: COMPETITIVE CRAFTERS, DROP-OFF DESPOTS, AND OTHER SUBURBAN SCOURGES* WHICH WAS A FINALIST FOR A GOODREADS READ-

ER'S CHOICE AWARD. HER LATEST BOOK IS *HOW I F*CKING DID IT: FROM MOVING ELVES TO MAKING OVER SIX-FIGURES ON THE INTERNET AND YOU CAN TOO.* SHE IS ALSO THE MASTERMIND BEHIND THE *NEW YORK TIMES* BESTSELLING *I JUST WANT TO PEE ALONE* SERIES. JOIN JEN'S 1+ MILLION FOLLOWERS ON SOCIAL MEDIA.

AFTERWORD

Thank you for reading this book! We really appreciate your support. If you could do us a huge favor and leave us a review everywhere you review books we'd be super grateful. Those reviews help us more than you can know.

If you know someone that might enjoy this book, please share your copy with them, or better yet, get them one!

ALSO AVAILABLE

I Just Want to Pee Alone

I Just Want to Be Alone

I STILL Just Want to Pee Alone

I Just Want to Be Perfect

But Did You Die?

You Do You!

Working with People I Want to Punch in the Throat: Cantankerous Clients, Micromanaging Minions, and Other Supercilious Scourges

People I Want to Punch in the Throat: Competitive Crafters, Drop-off Despots, and Other Suburban Scourges

Spending the Holidays with People I Want to Punch in the Throat: Yuletide Yahoos, Ho-Ho-Humblebraggers, and Other Seasonal Scourges

Made in the USA
Middletown, DE
23 April 2019